MALAYSIAN NATURE HANDBOOKS

General Editor

M. W. F. TWEEDIE

THE aim of the Malaysian Nature Handbooks is to provide a series of handy, well-illustrated guides to the fauna and flora of Malaysia and Singapore. They can, of course, be no more than introductory; the animal and plant life of Malaysia is on such a lavish scale that comprehensive accounts of the groups described in each of the Handbooks must be either severely technical or voluminous and correspondingly costly. The selection of species described in each one has been carefully made, however, to illustrate those most likely to be the first encountered by reasonably observant people residing in or visiting Malaysia and Singapore; reference to rarities or species confined to inaccessible country has been avoided, except where such species are of special interest.

It is the Editor's belief that interest in animals and plants is best aroused by providing the means of identifying and naming them. The emphasis of the Handbooks is therefore firstly on identification, but as much information on habits and biology is included as space will allow. It is hoped that they may be of use to schools in supplementing courses in nature study and biology, and a source of pleasure to that quite numerous assemblage of people whose complaint has been that they would gladly be naturalists if someone would show them the way.

OTHER TITLES IN THE SERIES
M. R. Henderson COMMON MALAYAN WILDFLOWERS
R. Morrell COMMON MALAYAN BUTTERFLIES
M. W. F. Tweedie COMMON BIRDS OF THE MALAY PENINSULA
B. M. Allen COMMON MALAYSIAN FRUITS

MALAYSIAN NATURE HANDBOOKS

Mammals of Malaysia

BY

M. W. F. TWEEDIE

Formerly Director of The Raffles Museum, Singapore

ILLUSTRATED BY MICHAEL J. WOODS

LONGMAN MALAYSIA

LONGMAN MALAYSIA SDN. BHD.
3, Jalan Kilang A, 46050 Petaling Jaya, Selangor Darul Ehsan.
Tel: 03-7920466, 7920803

*Associated companies, branches and representatives
throughout the world*

© M.W.F. Tweedie, text; 1978

All rights reserved. No part of this publication may be
reproduced, stored in a retrieval system, or transmitted
in any form or by any means, electronic, mechanical,
photocopying, recording or otherwise, without the
prior permission of the Copyright owner.

*First published 1978
Reprinted 1988*

ISBN 0 582 72424 4

Mammals of Malaysia

Printed by Vinlin Press Sdn. Bhd., Kuala Lumpur.

CONTENTS

INSECTIVORA	page	6
CHIROPTERA		11
DERMOPTERA		19
PRIMATES		20
PHOLIDOTA		28
RODENTIA		29
CARNIVORA		43
PROBOSCIDEA		56
PERISSODACTYLA		57
ARTIODACTYLA		59
SIRENIA		63
CETACEA		64
CHECKLIST		66

LIST OF PLATES

Plate 1 A COMMON TREESHREW
       B SHORT-TAILED MOLE
       C HOUSE SHREW
       D MOONRAT

     2 A LARGE FLYING FOX
       B HAIRLESS BAT
       C HORSFIELD'S FRUIT BAT

     3 A SLOW LORIS
       B WESTERN TARSIER
       C MALAYAN COLUGO

     4 A SPECTACLED LEAF MONKEY
       B LONG-TAILED MACAQUE
       C PIG-TAILED MACAQUE

     5 A WHITE-HANDED GIBBON
       B SIAMANG
       C ORANG-UTAN

     6 A RED-CHEEKED FLYING SQUIRREL
       B GREY-BELLIED SQUIRREL
       C PLANTAIN SQUIRREL
       D BLACK-BANDED SQUIRREL

     7 A, B RED GIANT FLYING SQUIRREL
       C BLACK GIANT SQUIRREL
       D PREVOST'S SQUIRREL

     8 A LONG-TAILED GIANT RAT
       B HOUSE RAT
       C SHREW-FACED GROUND SQUIRREL

     9 A LARGE BAMBOO RAT
       B MALAYAN PANGOLIN
       C MALAYAN PORCUPINE

Plate 10 A CLOUDED LEOPARD
       B DHOLE
       C MALAYAN SUN BEAR

    11 A, B PANTHER
        C   TIGER

    12 A SMALL-CLAWED OTTER
       B YELLOW-THROATED MARTEN
       C LEOPARD CAT

    13 A MASKED PALM CIVET
       B COMMON PALM CIVET
       C BINTURONG

    14 A SUMATRAN RHINOCEROS
       B GAUR
       C INDIAN ELEPHANT

    15 A BEARDED PIG
       B MALAYAN TAPIR
       C SAMBAR

    16 A LARGE MOUSE-DEER
       B BARKING DEER
       C SEROW

Each plate depicts animals of comparable size, but they are not drawn exactly to scale.

MAMMALS OF MALAYSIA

In common speech the word 'animal' is often restricted to mammals, but this leaves no word available to describe a member of the Animal Kingdom. To a zoologist fleas, fishes and pheasants are animals just as much as mice and men are: they are all living things which are not vegetables. A mammal can be defined as a warm-blooded vertebrate animal (that is possessing a backbone) that suckles its young with milk and is usually covered with a coat of hair. Almost all of them bear their young alive.

All Malaysian mammals, in fact all those native to Asia and Europe, belong to the dominant mammalian group called the placental mammals. The more primitive marsupials and monotremes are confined to the southern continents and southern North America. The monotremes are the extraordinary egg-laying platypus and echidna, only found in the Australian Region, and the marsupials are those whose young are born at a very early stage of development and transferred to a pouch on the outside of the mother's body: kangaroos and opossums are marsupials.

It is characteristic of the mammals that the mother not only feeds her young but also protects and educates them for a shorter or longer period, sometimes with the help of their father or of other members of a social group or herd. It is this that has led, during the course of evolution, to the mammals becoming the most highly developed and intelligent of all animals. The longer the period of growth to maturity, and consequently of education, the higher the level of mental development. The process culminates in our own species: we are just very advanced mammals.

Malaysia now comprises two distinct territories. The eleven states known collectively as Peninsular Malaysia bordered in the north by Thailand and south by Singapore plus the states of Sabah and Sarawak which occupy the north and north-eastern portion of the island of Borneo. In this book the two Malaysian territories will be referred to by the more explicit geographical terms Malaya and Borneo. Most of the smaller mammals described as common are found in Singapore.

Fig. 1. The geography of Sundaland: The ancient Sundaland, as indicated the present continental shelf, is surrounded by a broken line. The four large territories that comprise the modern 'Sundaland' of this book are named. Many smaller islands are included in Sundaland, among them Palawan, politically part of the Philippines.

The islands of Borneo, Sumatra and Java, together with the Malay Peninsula, stand on a shallow extension of the continental shelf. During the successive glacial periods or 'ice ages' or the Pleistocene Epoch, the most recent division of geological time ending about 10,000 years ago, this area was largely dry land, a great equatorial peninsula jutting out from south-eastern Asia. It has received the name 'Sundaland' and the fauna or assemblage of animals inhabiting it was distinctive, differing to some extent from that of continental Asia. The Malay Peninsula and the three islands retain many elements of this fauna, and I shall use the term Sundaland to define these four territories as they now are as well as for the old land area of which they are the partly submerged remains. The three islands are referred to as the Sunda Islands. Sulawesi (Celebes) and the so-called Lesser Sunda Islands, which extend eastward from Java, do not stand on the Sunda Shelf. The flooding and dividing up of Sundaland was a result of the world-wide rise in sea level after the latest of the glacial periods, due to the melting of the ice sheets and the return to the oceans of huge quantities of water.

The four territories comprising the present-day Sundaland are inhabited by faunas which have much in common, but that of Borneo is nevertheless distinctive, with about forty mammal species that are endemic; that is they exist nowhere else. Malaya has only two truly endemic species, a rat and a flying squirrel. The four bat species recorded only from Malaya are likely, on account of their mobility, to be found elsewhere in South-East Asia.

The marine mammals, whales and dolphins, that are seen in the seas surrounding Malaysia, have a distribution that is governed by quite different principles and most of them extend to the seas of the Indian and Pacific Oceans, or even of the whole world.

The natural condition of Malaysia, from which it has only recently emerged, is to be covered almost entirely with dense forest. It follows that the natural habitat of almost all the wild land mammals is rain forest or jungle. Most of them now inhabit what is left of this forest, from the leafy canopy of the tree tops to the jungle floor. A few have adapted more or less successfully to the artificial environment of plantations, villages and gardens created by man, but the majority will disappear if all the forest is destroyed.

We see far less of our wild mammals than of our birds because most mammals are nocturnal. They are enabled to be active at night partly by eyesight specially adapted for conditions of minimum light, partly by very acute senses of hearing and smell. Bats, which make up over a third of all the known species of Malaysian mammals, are almost all nocturnal; squirrels, on the other hand, are mostly animals of the day, and so are our most familiar wild mammals.

The classification of mammals, like that of other animals, is based on their supposed evolutionary history. On this basis the class Mammalia is divided into a number of orders, and these are the categories under which they will be described in this book; a family is a subdivision of an order. The English, Latin and Malay names are based on those used by Lord Medway in his *Wild Mammals of Malaya and offshore islands including Singapore* (O.U.P.) and his *Mammals of Borneo* published by the Malaysian Branch, Royal Asiatic Society. The Latin or zoological nomenclature provides all animals with two names, a specific one which identifies it precisely and a generic one which defines its closest relationship with other species. A group of animals included under one generic name is called a genus (plural genera); the word species is the same in singular and plural. The genus is put first and must have an inital capital letter, the species second without a capital; italic type is used for Latin names. Among the Malaysian squirrels is a number belonging to the genus *Callosciurus*, these include *Callosciurus prevostii* (Prevost's Squirrel) and *Callosciurus notatus* (Plantain Squirrel). Besides Lord Medway's books there are two useful smaller books by the late Professor J.L. Harrison. They are published by the local Nature Societies and have the titles *Introduction to the Mammals of Singapore and Malaya* and *Introduction to the Mammals of Sabah*.

The descriptions in this book include measurements in round figures of the length of the head and body together and of the tail; in bats the length of the forearm is useful in identification and this is also given. The metric scale is used with millimetres as the unit for small animals less than half a metre long, centimetres for larger ones and metres for the largest. A rat, head and body, is about 150 mm long, a cat 50 cm and a leopard about 1.3 metres. An inch is almost exactly $2\frac{1}{2}$ cm or 25 mm.

In these days we hear a great deal about conservation of wild life, and we must guard against any inclination to become tired or bored by the subject, which is of most urgent importance. Measures taken to promote conservation are of two kinds, preservation of the natural environment and legal protection for animals which appear to be in particular danger. The former is by far the most important of the two because it aims at preservation of all wild life, fauna and flora alike. It is useless to try to protect an animal if the habitat essential to its existence is completely destroyed. Maintenance of the National Parks and Reserves in Malaysia is of the utmost importance. If we cannot protect them from development and exploitation we shall be guilty of a crime of negligence and greed for which the world of the future will never forgive us.

In Peninsular Malaysia the Protection of Wildlife Act 1973 gives protection to many species of mammals and licences issued by the Game Department are necessary even for the common species. 78 per cent of Peninsular Malaysia's mammals are confined to primary and tall secondary forests and 81 per cent are restricted to areas below 600 metres; thus it is the lowland forests that are important to the continued survival of a large number of Malaysian mammals.

Legal measures, both against destruction of forest and hunting of rare animals, cannot be enforced effectively unless public opinion gives the law massive support. All naturalists realise this, and it is in the hope of encouraging those who are naturalists already, and perhaps of making some new ones, that this book has been written.

It could not have been written without the availability of Lord Medway's two books on the mammals of Malaya and Borneo and my thanks are also due to him for help and encouragement.

INSECTIVORA

The Insectivora are not, of course, the only mammals that feed on insects, but this diet is characteristic of them. They are the most primitive of the placental mammals and already existed in the Cretaceous Period when dinosaurs were the dominant land animals. Most of them are small and a species of shrew, found in Malaysia and widely distributed elsewhere, is the smallest known mammal. We also have in our fauna the largest of all the insectivores. The teeth are numerous with sharp points or cusps and many of the insectivores emit an unpleasant smell which protects them from being hunted and eaten by other animals.

The treeshrews (family Tupaiidae) are classified in most of the recent literature on mammals as primates, primitive relatives of the apes and monkeys. It is now considered that they are better regarded as a group of the Insectivora that have become specialised for climbing in trees and bushes. Nevertheless they are probably similar to the early insectivores from which the primates were derived by evolution.

MOONRAT OR GYMNURE *(Echinosorex gymnurus)*   Plate 1D

TIKUS AMBANG BULAN

Length 255–350 mm, tail 165–265 mm. Distribution Sundaland, except Java, Thailand and Burma. The moonrat is allied to the well known hedgehogs of temperate climates and is the world's largest insectivore. The black-and-white head and neck and particoloured tail are characteristic and are probably a pattern of warning coloration, as the appalling smell makes the animal quite inedible; it has been compared with acetylene gas, rotten garlic and stale sweat.

Moonrats are solitary animals, living on the forest floor and feeding on worms, snails, insects, freshwater crabs and the like. The animal hisses when frightened but is not known to make any other sound. Although active by day and night it is seldom seen, but is not uncommon in forest. The young are usually born two at a time.

Fig. 2. Lesser Gymnure.

LESSER GYMNURE *(Hylomys suillus)* Fig. 2

TIKUS BABI

Length 120–140 mm, tail very short, slender and hairless, around 20 mm. It is dark brown all over with a long pointed snout, and looks very like a large, rat-sized shrew. It is widespread in south-eastern Asia and is quite common in Malaysia at moderate heights in the mountains, where it is most often seen disappearing into a hole under a log. It lives on insects and its smell has been described as not quite as bad as that of its larger relative.

SHORT-TAILED MOLE *(Talpa micrura)* Plate 1B

TIKUS MENGGALI TANAH

Length about 120 mm. This is typical mole with the fore limbs greatly enlarged and strengthened for digging and the eyes reduced and overgrown with skin. The fur is velvetty black. It is widespread in eastern Asia but was unknown in Malaysia until 1937, when it was discovered on a tea estate in the Cameron Highlands. This is still the only Malaysian locality known for it and is the southern-most point of its range; it does not extend to Borneo.

Like other moles it spends almost all of its life in burrows not far below the surface of the soil, feeding on insects and earthworms. It must live in the forest but would be almost impossible to detect there. In the compacted soil of lawns and road verges slight rounded ridges are forced up over its more shallow burrows, and it is these that betray its presence.

House Shrew *(Suncus murinus)* Plate 1C

CENCURUT RUMAH

Length 100–150 mm, tail 70–95 mm. This rather large grey coloured shrew is widely distributed in Asia and lives as a commensal of man. That is to say it is a guest or lodger in our houses, paying for its keep by feeding on insects, especially cockroaches. It has a quite inoffensive musky smell and utters short, very shrill chirps when frightened. It is well known for its habit of keeping close to the wall of a room, never coming out into the open, and it is possible that it finds its way by echolocation in the way that will be described when we come to the bats. House shrews make a nest for breeding in outhouses or in grass in the open and have from one to five young at a time.

The genus *Suncus* is represented in Malaya and Borneo by another species, *Suncus etruscus* or SAVI'S PYGMY SHREW. It has a wide distribution from the Mediterranean region to Malaysia. It is found in a wide variety of habitats in this range but in Malaysia it only lives in forest. It is the smallest known mammal in the world: length about 40 mm, tail 25 mm, weight 1.8—2.4 g, about two-thirds of that of a Malaysian ten cent coin. Pygmy shrews are seldom seen but are probably not uncommon.

South-East Asian White-toothed Shrew *(Crocidura fuliginosa)*

CENCURUT HUTAN

Length 75–90 mm, tail 50–65 mm. Rather smaller than the house shrew with dark grey to black fur, this is the common shrew of the forest floor, scrub and grassland. It occurs in Malaya and Borneo and on the continent to north-west India. Like other shrews it feeds on insects.

All shrews eat great quantities of food in relation to their size and need food very frequently. Traps set for them must be inspected every two or three hours to save them from starving.

TREESHREWS

These are among the most interesting of the Malaysian mammals.

PLATE 1. A. Common Treeshrew; B. Short-tailed Mole; C. House Shrew; D. Moonrat.

PLATE 2. A. Large Flying Fox; B. Hairless Bat; C. Horsfield's Fruit Bat.

When they were first discovered they were regarded as belonging to the Insectivora, but were later transferred to the Primates, of which they were considered to be very primitive members, representative of what our own remote ancestors might have been like. Recently zoologists have put them back in the order Insectivora, but this in no way affects their status as interesting and primitive mammals. Their evolutionary origin seems to have been in Sundaland. About sixteen species are known, all from south-eastern Asia and India, of which ten live in Borneo, and of these six are endemic to the island. Three of the ten are found also in Malaya.

Treeshrews look remarkably like squirrels, so much so that the Malays use the same name, tupai, for both. They also resemble squirrels in being active by day. In the field treeshrews are distinguished from most squirrels by their pointed snouts and by the presence usually, of an oblique pale stripe on each shoulder. In the hand the presence of five clawed digits on the fore feet distinguishes them and their front or incisor teeth, unlike those of rodents, are pure white.

They climb well but live mainly among low trees and bushes and on the ground. Their diet is mixed, consisting of insects and also fruits and buds. Their breeding habits, so far as they are known, are peculiar. The male and female live together in a nest made in a hole in a log or some similar site, and the young, numbering two or three, are placed in a separate nest made for them by the female. In this nest she visits them only once every two days, giving them at each visit an enormous meal of thick milk. The visits last about five minutes, so the young get very little parental attention and care. Treeshrews will breed in captivity only if two nest boxes are provided for each pair.

COMMON TREESHREW *(Tupaia glis)* Plate 1A

TUPAI MUNCUNG BESAR

Length 135–205 mm, tail 125–195 mm. Back and tail brown, underparts and the oblique shoulder stripe paler and reddish. The LESSER TREESHREW *(Tupaia minor)* is rather smaller and dull white below. These are the two species of *Tupaia* found in Malaya as well as Borneo. The LARGE TREESHREW *(Tupaia tana)* is a little larger than *T. glis* and is confined to Borneo and Sumatra. It has a black central dorsal stripe which is bordered with buff and black on the neck.

PENTAIL TREESHREW *(Ptilocercus lowii)*   Fig. 3
TUPAI AKAR MALAM
Length 130–140 mm, tail 165–190 mm. Found in Malaya, Borneo and Sumatra, this animal is quite unlike the other treeshrews and immediately distinguished by the tail. This is naked for most of its length and has a flat feather-like growth of long white hairs on each side near the tip. The pentail treeshrew is nocturnal and much more completely arboreal than the other treeshrews, seldom coming to the ground. It lives entirely on insects and is one of Malaysia's more rare and peculiar mammals.

Fig. 3. Pentail Treeshrew.

CHIROPTERA
BATS

In the environment of tropical rain forest bats are the most varied and successful order of mammals. Nearly a hundred species have been recorded from Malaya and Borneo of which about fifty are common to the two territories. This amounts to more than a third of the whole mammal fauna. Bats are difficult to collect and study and no doubt more species will be discovered in our area. They are the only mammals that can fly and their wings consist of a membrane of skin supported by the fore limbs and elongated fingers. The membrane continues to the ankle and is usually continued between the hind limbs, where it is called the interfemoral membrane. The degree to which this is developed and the way in which the tail is involved in it afford characters useful in bat classification. The first digit or thumb of the fore limb is clawed and is used for climbing and scrambling about: some bats have a claw on the second digit as well, arising from the front edge of the wing. As they are involved with the wings the hind limbs cannot be used to stand or run; bats can only crawl and climb and hang.

They owe their success to the fact that they have mastered the art of flying at night; birds, which depend on their sense of sight, have had only limited success in this field of activity. The bats have succeeded by making themselves independent of daylight, directing themselves and locating their surroundings by using ultrasonic sound waves instead of the electromagnetic waves that we and most other animals perceive as light. They provide their own sound waves by emitting from their nostrils short pulses of ultrasonic sound which is reflected from objects near to the bat. It hears and interprets these reflected echoes so precisely that it can locate and capture a flying moth or fly through a quite small aperture. Bats can be caught in 'mist nets' with threads too fine to give an echo.

The order Chiroptera is divided into two suborders, the Megachiroptera and the far more numerous Microchiroptera. The former are the fruit bats, and include the largest kinds; the latter are mainly small and most of them feed on insects. It is in the Microchiroptera that the faculty of echo-sounding is highly developed. The fruit bats have large efficient eyes and fly at dusk and dawn as well as at night.

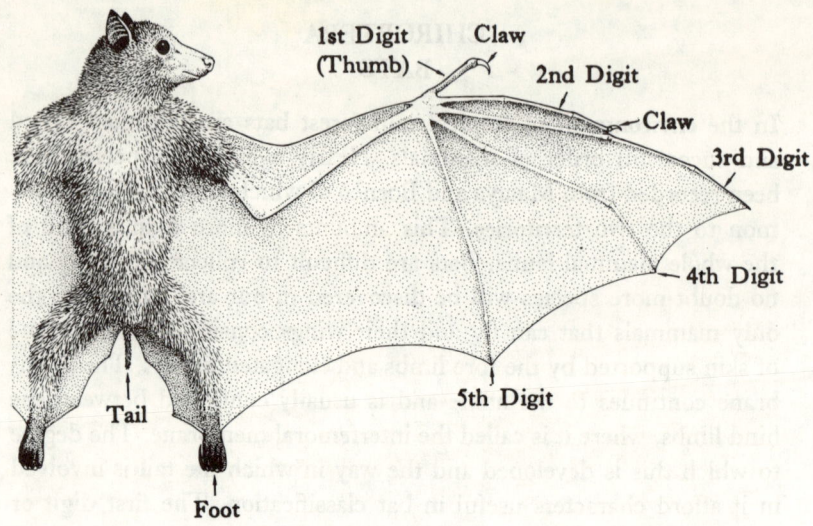
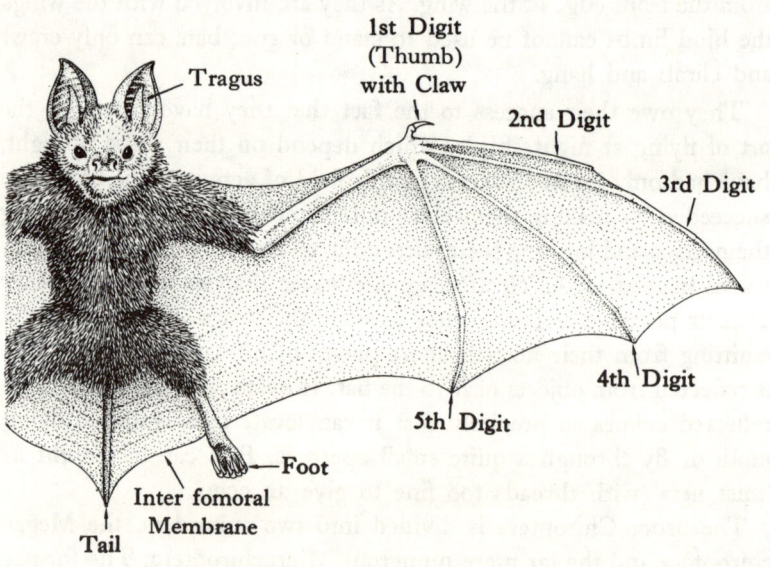

Fig. 4. Principal features of bats. Above a fruit bat; below a common or Vespertilionid bat. Note the presence of two claws on the wing of the fruit bat.

We have space to describe only a few of the Malaysian bats, those most likely to be seen or species of particular interest. The forearm measurements are easy to take on a dead or captured bat and they give an idea of the relative sizes of the different species. All those described range more or less widely outside Malaysia and, with one exception, are found in Malaya and Borneo.

MEGACHIROPTERA OR FRUIT BATS

The most obvious feature that distinguishes this suborder of bats is the presence of a claw on the second digit as well as on the thumb, so that there are two claws on the leading edge of the wing. Among Malaysian fruit bats there are only two exceptions to this, the cave fruit bat and its relative the Dulit fruit bat, which is rare and restricted to Borneo. They also have normal mammalian heads with fairly long muzzles, large eyes and small ears lacking any accessory lobes or flaps. The tail is very short or lacking and the interfemoral membrane is no more than a fringe of skin on the hind legs. The largest bats are included in this group and none of them is very small.

LARGE FLYING FOX *(Pteropus vampyrus)*   Plate 2A

KELUANG

Forearm 185–200 mm. This is the largest bat in the world, with a wingspread of up to 1.5 metres or nearly five feet. The nape and shoulders are orange-brown, the rest of the body dark brown.

    Flying foxes roost by day in crowds in trees, sometimes hundreds together. Shortly before dusk they fly away to feed and return before daybreak. Their feeding place may be flowering or fruiting jungle trees, or it may be a rambutan orchard, in which case a great deal of damage is done. In captivity they feed freely on fruit and become very tame. As is the rule among bats one young is born at a time and is carried for several days by the mother and then left at the roost when its parent goes out to feed.

    The ISLAND FLYING FOX *(Pteropus hypomelanus)* is similar but smaller and is confined to offshore islands all round the Malaysian coasts, though they may fly to the mainland to feed.

Malaysian Fruit Bat *(Cynopterus brachyotis)*

CECADU PISANG

Forearm 52–72 mm. Much smaller than the flying foxes and the commonest of the fruit bats. The fur is brown to greyish brown, adults may be yellow round the shoulders and throat and the ears are edged with white. Also the bones and tendons of the fingers show white through the upper surface of the wing membrane. It roosts in trees and sometimes in houses and verandahs and brings fruit to its roost to be eaten. Horsfield's Fruit Bat *(Cynopterus horsfieldi)* shown on plate 2, is very similar but a little larger, forearm 70–78 mm.

Cave Fruit Bat *(Eonycteris spelaea)*

CECADU GUA

Forearm 62–71 mm. No claw on the second digit of the hand, but a typical small fruit bat with dark brown fur and a long pointed muzzle. It roosts only in caves and there is a large colony in the Batu Caves at Kuala Lumpur. Its natural food consists chiefly of nectar and pollen from flowers.

The Common Long-tongued Fruit Bat *(Macroglossus lagochilus)*, forearm 40–43 mm, has an even longer muzzle and a long tongue with a brush-like tip. These are specialisations for feeding on nectar, and these bats play an important part as pollinators of flowers. This species is common in mangrove swamps.

Geoffroy's Rousette *(Rousettus amplexicaudatus)*

CECADU BESAR

Forearm 72–87 mm. Dark brown all over the body and wings, a little larger than the cave fruit bat and distinguished from it by having a claw on the second digit. From another cave dweller, Horsfield's fruit bat, the rousette is distinguished by the uniform dark brown wings and ears. It roosts in caves and is of interest because it has developed a form of echo-location comparable with that of the Microchiroptera, but less refined and produced in a different way, and certainly evolved separately. Its basis is a high-pitched buzzing call made by vibrating the tongue against the palate. The rousette is widespread but nowhere very common.

MICROCHIROPTERA OR INSECTIVOROUS BATS

This group comprises by far the greater number of species. Of those whose feeding habits are known all the Malaysian species except one feed on insects, the exception being a predator on other bats and small birds. Their dependence on echo-location has led to modification of the ears and in some genera of the area of the face round the nose. The ears are generally larger than in fruit bats and all but the horseshoe bats have a cartilaginous projection inside the ear called the tragus; in the horseshoe bats its place seems to be taken by the antitragus, a lobe of the outer edge of the ear. In the horseshoe bats and false vampires there are folds and frills of skin around the nose which are believed to enable the bat to direct and beam its pulses of ultra-sound and so enhance the efficiency of the echo-location system. It is these so-called noseleaves that make the faces of bats possessing them so very ugly by human standards.

The largest of the microchiropteran bats are about as big as the rousette, but nowhere near as large as a flying fox. Most of them are small and the smallest are quite tiny mammals. They can be sorted into groups by the presence or absence of noseleaves and tragus and by the arrangement of the tail and interfemoral membrane.

A. WITH NOSELEAVES

1. HORSESHOE BATS. The grotesquely developed noseleaves and short ears without any tragus are characteristic of these bats; there is an antitragus on the margin of the ear. In most species there is a tail enclosed for its whole length by the interfemoral membrane. The largest of them are exceeded in size among Malaysian bats only by the flying foxes. There is a number of species distinguished by the structure of the noseleaves and other details beyond the scope of this book.

COMMON ROUNDLEAF HORSESHOE BAT *(Hipposideros galeritus)*

KELAWAR LADAM BULAT GUA

Forearm 46–51 mm. This is the commonest horseshoe bat and large numbers are found roosting in limestone caves. Fur dark brown above, paler below. The DIADEM ROUNDLEAF HORSESHOE BAT *(Hipposideros diadema*) is one of the largest species, forearm 85–90 mm. Adults are golden brown with paler marks on the shoulders and sides. This is another quite common cave bat.

Fig. 5. Face of Diadem Roundleaf Horseshoe Bat.

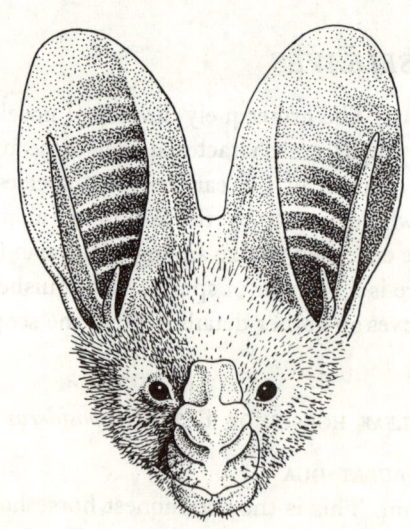

Fig. 6. Face of Malayan False Vampire.

2. FALSE VAMPIRES. The noseleaf is prominent but smaller than that of horseshoe bats. The ears are large and rounded and joined together with skin over the top of the head; they have a tragus divided into two unequal lobes. An interfemoral membrane is present but no tail.

MALAYAN FALSE VAMPIRE *(Megaderma spasma)* Fig. 6

KELAWAR TELINGA LEBAR

Forearm 54–61 mm. Characters as above, fur grey or dull brown. This bat roosts in caves and sometimes in tunnels or culverts and feeds on large insects. These are carried to feeding roosts, which are usually not the same as the daytime resting place. The INDIAN FALSE VAMPIRE *(Megaderma lyra)* is larger and is carnivorous, preying on birds and other bats, and has been known to pick captured small bats out of a mist net. It is a continental species, occurring in northern Malaya but not in Borneo.

B. WITHOUT NOSELEAVES

1. SHEATH-TAILED BATS AND TOMB BATS. In this group the basal half of the tail is enclosed in the interfemoral membrane and the distal half protrudes and lies on the surface of the membrane. The name 'tomb bat' refers to the habit of some of these bats of roosting by day in ancient tombs in Egypt and nearby countries.

BLACK-BEARDED TOMB BAT *(Taphozous melanopogon)*

KELAWAR DAGU HITAM

Forearm 63–68 mm. The fur is rather pale brown and adult males have a patch of long blackish hairs on the throat. This is mainly a cave dweller and roosts in the Bat Temple at Penang, and sometimes in houses.

2. COMMON OR VESPERTILIONID BATS. The tail is slender and is enclosed in the interfemoral membrane. The majority of the Malaysian bats belong to this family, and we can do no more than mention a few common or interesting species.

House Bat *(Scotophilus kuhlii)*

KELAWAR RUMAH

Forearm 47–54 mm. A medium-sized bat with sleek brown fur that roosts in colonies, often in the roofs of houses or in the crowns of palm trees. It is common in towns.

Malaysian Noctule *(Pipistrellus stenopterus)*

KELAWAR MALAM

Forearm 38–42 mm. A common species with reddish brown fur that roosts in the roofs of houses in rural areas or in hollow trees. It is a Sundaland animal, confined to Malaya, Sumatra and Borneo and some nearby islands. The Latin name *Nyctalus stenopterus* has been used for it in the past.

Whiskered Bat *(Myotis mystacinus)*

KELAWAR DAUN PISANG

Forearm 35–38 mm. An ordinary looking small greyish brown bat that in Malaysia has the habit of roosting in the rolled central leaves of banana plants. In contrast with the last species it has a remarkably wide range, from Europe, including Britain, right across Asia and southward to New Guinea.

Lesser Flat-headed Bat *(Tylonycteris pachypus)*

KELAWAR BULUH KECIL

Forearm 35–40 mm. The fur is reddish brown, the flight membrane dark brown and there are disc-like pads on the wrists and on the soles of the hind feet. The skull is extraordinarily flattened. This little bat and its slightly larger relative *Tylonycteris robustula* are common where bamboo grows and they are associated with the plant by their habit of roosting inside the stems. They get in through vertical slits made by stem-boring beetle larvae and the smaller species can squeeze through a slit only 3.6 mm wide. Normally two young are born, an exceptional condition among bats.

3. FREE-TAILED BATS. The tail is rather long and thick and protrudes for the whole of its length with the interfemoral membrane loosely folded at its base.

WRINKLE-LIPPED BAT *(Tadarida plicata)*

KELAWAR RUMAH

Forearm 43–47 mm. The ears are joined over the head by a web of skin. This feature and the tail, together with the dark brown fur, make this fairly small bat easy to recognise. It is widespread and common and roosts in caves and buildings, sometimes in large colonies.

HAIRLESS BAT *(Cheiromeles torquatus)*   Plate 2B

BATIN KELASAR

Forearm 80–86 mm. This is the largest of the few members of this group and is an unmistakeable and somewhat ugly animal. It has a blunt snout, rather large round ears and is covered with loose folded almost black skin. This is naked except for a little hair round a gland on the throat and some bristles on the first toe of the hind foot. When it is hanging at rest the wing-tips are folded and tucked into pockets of skin on each flank.

It normally rests in hollow trees, but sometimes in caves, and there is a well known colony in the Great Cave at Niah in Sarawak. The bat is associated in a curious way with large semi-parasitic earwigs of the genus *Arixenia*. There are two species, one of which feeds on material scraped from the surface of the bats skin, the other lives below the roost feeding on its dung. In spite of its unattractive appearance the hairless bat is relished as food by some of the aboriginal people.

DERMOPTERA
COLUGOS or FLYING LEMURS

Colugo is a better name for these animals than flying lemur as they have no particular relation with lemurs. There are only two known species, one inhabiting the Philippines, the other more widespread in South-East Asia and Sundaland. Their classification is a zoological puzzle, for they have no close relation with any other known mammals, living or extinct. They have a membrane of skin, covered with fur, which extends from the throat back to include all four limbs and the tail, so that it surrounds the body except for the head. This enables colugos to glide among the trees just as flying squirrels do.

MALAYAN COLUGO *(Cynocephalus variegatus)* Plate 3C
KUBUNG

Length 320–380 mm, tail around 250 mm. The upper parts are grey or reddish brown mottled and streaked with black and white, a pattern that closely simulates the bark of a tree. The claws are strong and sharp and the animal climbs actively, but rather awkwardly, and hangs upside-down from all four feet on small branches. The tail is carried folded under the belly. In gliding the limbs and tail are extended outward and the membrane tightly stretched between them. From a fair height distances between 50 and 100 metres are easily covered.

The Malayan colugo lives both in the hills and the lowlands and is not uncommon. It seems able to exist well in secondary forest and even among coconut palms. They rest during the day, well camouflaged by the grey or brown streaky fur, and become active in the evening, feeding from then on into the night. The food is leaves and shoots, but they will not live in captivity, whether captured young or adult, so no attempt should ever be made to catch and keep them. One young is born at a time and carried by the mother clinging to her underside and enclosed in the flying membrane when she is in the usual upside-down resting position.

PRIMATES

As we ourselves belong to this order of mammals we naturally regard the primates as the most highly evolved of all animals. They include, as well as man, apes, monkeys and various lemur-like animals, two of which are found in Malaysia. Strictly speaking, the term 'lemur' should be used only for a group of primates confined to Madagascar.

PLATE 3. A. Slow Loris; B. Western Tarsier; C. Malayan Colugo.

PLATE 4. A. Spectacled Leaf Monkey; B. Long-tailed Macaque; C. Pig-tailed Macaque.

PLATE 5. A. White-handed Gibbon; B. Siamang; C. Orang-utan.

PLATE 6. A. Red-cheeked Flying Squirrel; B. Grey-bellied Squirrel; C. Plantain Squirrel; D. Black-banded Squirrel.

Most of the primates are active by day and climb among trees. This has led to the fore limbs becoming adapted for grasping and to the eyes being directed forwards for binocular vision, because ability to judge distance is essential for active climbing. The combination of grasping hands and efficient eyes has led in its turn to the habit of manipulating and examining objects, and this, it is argued, to a sense of curiosity and a high level of intelligence.

Primates are believed to have evolved from some sort of climbing member of the Insectivora, probably not unlike a treeshrew, through stages represented today by the lemur-like animals, the monkeys, apes and finally man. In Malaysia we are fortunate in having all these stages represented in the living fauna, a sort of spectrum of primate evolution unequalled in any other area.

THE LEMUR-LIKE PRIMATES, LORIS AND TARSIER

SLOW LORIS *(Nycticebus coucang)* Plate 3A

KONGKANG

Length 270–300 mm, tail rudimentary. The grey-brown fur, big eyes, spectacle-marked face and general 'teddy bear' appearance make the loris unmistakeable; its slow movements are also characteristic. It is found all over Sundaland and north to Indo-China and the eastern Himalayas.

It is active at night and sleeps during the day, hence the very large eyes. It lives climbing slowly about among trees and bushes, never jumping, always holding on with at least one limb. It can, however, make a very rapid snatch to catch an insect or small lizard. Most of its natural food is of this kind but it will also eat fruit. Both fore and hind feet are hand-like with the thumb and great toe opposed to the other digits. All of these have flat nails except the second digit of the hind foot, which has a claw that is used to comb and groom the fur. In Malaysia the loris is totally protected and it is illegal to kill them or take them into captivity. Usually only one young is born, fully furred and with its eyes open. It lives clinging to its mother until it is weaned.

WESTERN TARSIER *(Tarsius bancanus)* Plate 3B
KERA HANTU

Length rather variable, around 300 mm, tail as long as the body. Confined to Borneo and Sumatra. Two other species are found in the Philippines and Sulawesi (Celebes) respectively. The Malay name 'ghost monkey' well describes the tarsier, though it is much smaller than any ordinary monkey. Its fur is light brown and the tail is naked except for a tuft of hair at the tip. The ears are large, the eyes enormous and the hind legs much longer and stronger than the fore legs. The fingers and toes have adhesive pads, rather like those of a tree-frog, and the nails are much reduced.

When at rest tarsiers usually cling to a vertical twig or branch. They are wholly nocturnal and feed on insects and other small animals and they move about by making powerful standing jumps of two metres or more like a frog or a grasshopper. Their huge eyes give them the necessary night vision for this activity and they live in thick forest and can only be seen by hunting at night with a torch or lantern. The nose of a tarsier is dry like that of a man or a monkey; lorises have a wet nose like a dog or a cat. This is important because it places the tarsier a few rungs higher on the ladder of primate evolution than the loris.

MONKEYS

These animals are much more advanced than the loris and tarsier. They are larger, live longer and their children grow more slowly and are better educated. Most of them live in groups with a leader and senior and junior members, and the young have to learn how to fit into a small community of this kind as well as to find their food and avoid their enemies. All the Malaysian species are more or less arboreal and both hands and feet are adapted for grasping and climbing. There are two distinct groups, the macaques, which spend much of their time on the ground and are omnivorous, and the leaf monkeys, relatives of the Indian langur, which seldom descend from the trees and feed entirely on leaves.

Long-tailed Macaque *(Macaca fascicularis)*   Plate 4B

KERA

Length 35–45 cm, tail 40–55 cm. Widespread in south-eastern Asia and Sundaland. The greyish brown fur and long tail distinguish this monkey, which is by far the commonest species in Malaysia. Its communal groups range from about 8 to as many as 40 in number, and they are seen in all types of country, from the hills to the sea shore; they swim quite well. In places like the Botanic Gardens, Penang, they become very bold and tame. They occasionally hunt crabs in mangrove swamp, and the rather inappropriate name 'crab-eating macaque' is sometimes used for this monkey. They are in fact quite omnivorous and may be a pest in paddy fields and gardens. When disturbed they utter a warning call, k'rrah, k'rrah, of which the Malay name is a rendering.

In captivity they thrive on a mixed diet of the sort of food we eat ourselves, and one has been recorded as living 27 years. But they do not make pleasant pets as they are destructive and have unreliable tempers. Usually one young is born and is carried underneath the mother until it is weaned.

Pig-tailed Macaque *(Macaca nemestrina)*   Plate 4C

BERUK

Length up to 60 cm, tail one third of length and generally held half erect and curved. Found wild in Sundaland (except Java) and south-eastern Asia. This is a large thickset monkey with brown fur and a pinkish brown face. Size, colour and the short tail immediately distinguish it from the long-tailed macaque, and it is less arboreal, though it climbs very well. It lives in small groups and is sometimes solitary.

This is the monkey that is trained to climb coconut palms and twist off the nuts. They ride on the carrier of the master's bicycle and are never free but work always with a collar and a long cord. Some of them were trained by a Singapore botanist to climb the great forest trees and throw down samples of leaves, flowers and fruit; he maintains that he could not have written his book on Malayan trees without their help. Never approach or try to touch a domesticated beruk; they are formidable and dangerous animals.

A similar but rather smaller monkey, the STUMP-TAILED MACAQUE *(Macaca speciosa)* ranges from the continent just into northern Malaya. It has a very short tail and a blotched red face.

LEAF MONKEYS (genus *Presbytis*) Plate 4A

LOTONG, CENGKUNG, CENEKA

Six species of these monkeys are found in Malaysia, one in Malaya but not Borneo, three in Borneo but not Malaya and two in both territories. Leaf monkeys are strictly vegetarian animals that live high up in the trees. They are mostly a bit bigger than a long-tailed macaque and have very long tails, one-and-a-half times the length of the body. They have large stomachs due to internal adaptations for digesting leaves, but this in no way affects their agility in climbing and jumping among the branches. The fingers are long, the thumb short and the fur is shaggy and often stands up as a crest above or around the head. Most of them are grey, one species varies from grey or brown to black and the MAROON LEAF MONKEY of Borneo *(Presbytis rubicunda)* has bright reddish-brown fur. The young, when they are small, usually differ rather conspicuously from the adult. Those of the SILVERED LEAF MONKEY *(Presbytis cristata)* are bright orange contrasting surprisingly with their dull grey parents.

The commonest species in Malaya is the BANDED LEAF MONKEY *(Presbytis melalophos)*. This is the variously coloured species, usually dark above, paler beneath and on the thighs. The young are pale grey with a dark cap and dorsal stripe. This and the Silvered Leaf Monkey are the two species common to Malaya and Borneo. The SPECTACLED LEAF MONKEY *(Presbytis obscura)* ranges into Malaya from the north and does not extend to Borneo. It is fairly common and distinguished by conspicuous white rings round the eyes; the juveniles are pale orange or buff.

The Banded Leaf Monkey has a harsh, rattling alarm call and the other species have distinctive calls made up of grunts, snorts, clucking and squeaking. They will live in captivity on a diet of fresh leaves from the vegetable garden, beans, carrots and soft fruit, but are not recommended as pets.

PROBOSCIS MONKEY *(Nasalis larvatus)* Fig. 7

LOTONG BANGKATAN, KERA BELANDA

Length 50–60 cm, tail a little longer. The fur is reddish brown, the arms, legs, tail and a ruff on the neck usually white, the head with a cap of thick reddish hair. The skin of the face is red and the nose grotesquely enlarged, long and drooping in the adult male, short and upturned in females and young. This odd-looking animal is confined to the coastal swamps of Borneo and is really a leaf monkey that has taken to living in mangrove swamps, and it feeds almost entirely on the leaves of one kind of tree called *Sonneratia*. They swim readily

Fig. 7. Proboscis Monkey, adult male.

and often drop off quite high branches into the water. The adult males make a deep honking noise in which the nose seems to be involved as it straightens out with each honk, but the purpose of the enlarged nose is not yet understood.

APES

Apes and monkeys are often confused, but are quite distinct groups of animals. Apes are our nearest relatives in the Animal Kingdom and have more highly developed brains and level of intelligence than monkeys. They share with us the feature of being without a tail; all Malaysian monkeys have a tail, usually long and always obvious. Also the two climb differently: monkeys run and scramble about among the branches, using all four limbs, while apes hang and swing from branch to branch by means of their arms.

There are four distinct kinds of apes in the world, the chimpanzee and gorilla of Africa and the orang-utan and gibbons of Asia. Both of the latter live in Malaysia and all the Malaysian apes are protected by law. They must not be hunted or killed nor may they be kept in captivity without a license.

WHITE-HANDED GIBBON *(Hylobates lar)* Plate 5A
WA-WA

Length around 46 cm; widely distributed in Malaya and countries to the north of it. The fur varies from black to buff or cream colour; the hands and feet are white, an obvious feature in a black wa-wa but difficult to make out in an almost white one. The face is black with a ring of white hair around it.

Gibbons live in family groups, usually a mated pair and two or three offspring of different ages, but unmated adults may lead solitary lives. Their home is in the jungle canopy, the tops of the trees, where they normally progress by swinging from branch to branch by their long arms, hurling themselves across perilous looking spaces as they go from tree to tree. They are mostly vegetarian, eating fruit and leaves and a certain amount of animal food such as insects. Their voice is a loud, wonderfully musical hooting or shouting, familiar to everyone who has spent only a little time in the Malaysian forests.

One young is born and is carried by the mother until weaned at 4 to 7 months; maturity is reached at 6 to 8 years.

There are two other very similar Malaysian gibbons, the DARK-HANDED or AGILE GIBBON (*Hylobates agilis*), which has hands and feet the same colour as the body and is found in northern Malaya and certain parts of Borneo, and the BORNEAN GIBBON (*Hylobates muelleri*), confined to Borneo.

Gibbons make attractive pets if captured young, but to catch a young one you have to murder its mother. Often the young one gets killed too, so for every pet gibbon a number of wild ones have sacrificed their lives. They are protected by law, but in any case no humane person should ever encourage the trade in them by buying or keeping one. In the wild they can only live in high forest. If all the forest is destroyed the beautiful singing gibbons will be lost forever.

SIAMANG *(Hylobates syndactylus)* Plate 5B

SIAMANG

Length 75–90 cm, and stands about a metre high. Confined to Malaya and Sumatra in high forest of the hills and foothills, this is the largest of the gibbons and entirely black, face and fur alike. The second and third digits of the hind foot are joined by a web of skin, and there is a sac on the front of the throat which is blown up like a balloon when the animal is calling. The voice is a combination of whooping and a deep booming note which has tremendous carrying power. They live and feed like the other gibbons, some as solitary bachelors and spinsters, some in family groups which establish territories and guard them jealously.

ORANG-UTAN *(Pongo pygmaeus)* Plate 5C

MAWAS

A large ape with about the bulk of a man, confined to Borneo and Sumatra. Fur coarse, shaggy and rather sparse, arms longer and stronger than the legs with a span of over two metres. Old males develop fleshy lobes on each side of the face and a pouch under the chin. The English name is derived from the Malay language (man of the forest) but is not the name by which the Malays know the animal.

They live among the trees but are too heavy to perform the sort of acrobatics that gibbons do, though they can easily hang by one or both arms. They are much less sociable than most other primates; the males and females meet only briefly and the only lasting relationship is between mother and young. These are not weaned until they are two years old, become mature at about 8 years and are known to live to an age of 40. Their ability to lead an independent life in the wild is largely a matter of education imparted by the mother; a tame one released and abandoned in the jungle will soon die. They make platforms of interwoven branches to sleep on at night and their food is fruit and succulent shoots.

Captive orang-utans command a high price, not so much as pets but for zoos and as experimental animals. As in the case of gibbons capture of young ones can only be effected by killing adults and the incidental killing of young as well. Their numbers are now much reduced and they are protected, more or less effectively, both in Malaysia and Indonesia. Efforts are also made to train surrendered and confiscated pet orang-utans to live in the wild. Their continued existence depends on the preservation of extensive areas of primary forest.

PHOLIDOTA
PANGOLINS

MALAYAN PANGOLIN *(Manis javanica)* Plate 9B

TENGGILING

Length, including tail, around 85 cm. Found in south-eastern Asia, Sundaland and the Philippines. The size, shape and body covering of brown scales make this animal unmistakeable. The scales are formed of modified hair and there is normal hair between the scales and underneath the body. The pangolin is not uncommon in forest and is sometimes seen in plantations and even gardens. It is wholly toothless and its food is ants and termites which it picks up with its long sticky tongue. Its fore feet and claws are very powerful and it uses them to dig out the insects on which it feeds. It lives mainly on the ground but can climb well, making use of its muscular prehensile tail. When alarmed it curls up, wrapping its armoured tail over its head. One young is born which rides on its mother's back, just in front of the tail, while it is small. In Malaysia this animal is totally protected by law.

There are seven known species of pangolins or scaly anteaters, found in Africa and the warmer parts of Asia. Their relationship with other mammals is unknown and they are classified entirely on their own.

RODENTIA
RODENTS

Rodents are found all over the world in great variety, and they make up about two-fifths of all the known mammal species. In Malaysia there are more bats than rodents, but the latter are also so numerous that we can only mention a selection of them.

They are almost all small animals and their most characteristic feature is the form and arrangement of their teeth. They all have two chisel-like incisor teeth at the front of the upper and lower jaw. These continue growing throughout the animal's life and are kept at a constant size by continuous wear at their tips. Behind these incisors there is a long gap and then a set of chewing or grinding molar teeth. In this gap the cheeks can be drawn together shutting off the back part of the mouth, so that the incisors can be used either in feeding or for purposes not connected with eating, such as fighting, digging, gnawing through obstacles or chopping up nesting material. The food, mainly vegetable, is cut off with the incisors and passed to the back of the mouth to be chewed and swallowed. Their teeth, together with their handy front paws, provide them with a sort of tool-kit of great efficiency, and no doubt this is the key to their success.

In Asia they fall conveniently into three groups: squirrels, rats and mice, and porcupines, all well represented in Malaysia.

SQUIRRELS

Squirrels deserve fuller treatment in a book of this kind than the other numerous and diverse gropus of mammals because most of them are active by day and so are the mammals most often seen.

Since they depend greatly on their own sense of sight they develop distinctive colour patterns for recognition by members of their own species, and these also serve to make them relatively easy for us to identify them. In both these respects they resemble birds and they have been called 'bird-watcher's mammals'. We have space to mention about half of the 40-odd species known to live in Malaysia.

We will look first at some of the typical squirrels that climb about by day among the trees. Their habits are fairly uniform and need not be repeated for each species. They are mainly vegetable feeders but take some insect food, and for breeding they make round nests, with a hole on one side, of leaves, bark and fibres.

PLANTAIN SQUIRREL *(Callosciurus notatus)* Plate 6C
TUPAI PINANG, TUPAI MERAH

Length 150–220 mm, tail nearly as long. Brown above, belly red and a buff-over-black stripe on each side. Voice a shrill chatter and also single chirps, each accompanied by a jerk of the tail. This is the common squirrel of gardens, plantations and lowland forest in Borneo and southern and central Malaya.

MOUNTAIN RED-BELLIED SQUIRREL *(Callosciurus flavimanus)*
TUPAI BUKIT

Size similar to plantain squirrel. Brown above and along the middle of the belly, sides of the belly chestnut red; no buff-and-black band on the flanks. Voice a hoarse 'chuk-chuk' and a rattling alarm note. Seen commonly in the Malayan mountains above 1000 metres, not in Borneo. Formerly known as *C. erythraeus*.

GREY-BELLIED SQUIRREL *(Callosciurus caniceps)* Plate 6B
TUPAI TERATUK

Size similar to plantain squirrel. Brown above washed with reddish on the back, grey below, no buff-and-black stripe on the flanks. Voice a loud harsh chuckle and also a repeated bird-like 'cheep' accompanied by jerking of the tail. Common in plantations, gardens and secondary forests in Malaya especially so in the north. It extends into Malaya from the north and does not occur in Borneo.

BLACK-BANDED SQUIRREL *(Callosciurus nigrovittatus)* Plate 6D

TUPAI TOMPOK

Size a little larger than the plantain squirrel. Brown above, grey below, with a buff-over-black stripe on each flank like that of the plantain squirrel (but that species is red below). Voice the usual chattering and chirping and sometimes a longer shrill call. It inhabits lowland forest in Malaya and Borneo.

Ear-spot Squirrel *(Callosciurus adamsi)*

TUPAI TELINGA KUNING

Size a little smaller than the plantain squirrel, which it resembles (red belly, buff-and-black side stripes) but is distinguished by having a buff spot behind each ear. Rare and confined to the lowlands of Borneo.

PREVOST'S SQUIRREL *(Callosciurus prevostii)* Plate 7D

TUPAI GADING

Length 240–260 mm, tail nearly as long. Distinctly larger than the five species already described. In Malaya it is black above, including the top of the head and the tail, and the belly and legs are deep chestnut red. On each side, from the nose to the base of the tail, is a broad white stripe which may be interrupted at the shoulder by extension of the red on the fore leg. In Borneo it varies in the extent of the white stripe. This may be developed as in the Malayan form; it may be reduced to a faint pale streak or be absent, so that the squirrel is black and red; or it may expand dorsally to cover the head and fore part of the back.

This beautiful squirrel inhabits lowland forest, but is sometimes seen on plantations, especially oil palm estates. It feeds on the fruit but is never common enough to do serious damage.

SLENDER SQUIRREL *(Sundasciurus tenuis)*

TUPAI CERLEH

Length 115–150 mm, tail usually rather less and thinly haired. Upperparts and limbs brown, tail darker, underparts greyish buff. Rather like the grey-bellied squirrel (which is only seen in northern Malaya) but distinctly smaller. Voice a shrill double chirp, 'chewit, chewit'. Common in Malaya and Borneo in mountain and lowland forest and also scrub and bushland. It is usually seen in small groups of two to five.

HIMALAYAN STRIPED SQUIRREL *(Tamiops macclellandii)*
TUPAI BUNGA

Length 90–105 mm, tail 85–100 mm. There is a central black stripe along the back and on each side of it two more black stripes separated by yellow ones; sides, head and tail brown with a patch of white at the base of the ear; belly orange. The voice is a shrill chirp. A little smaller than the slender squirrel, this pretty little animal extends into Malaya from the north and is confined to the mountains. It is not found in any of the Sunda Islands.

In Borneo, and restricted to the island, there are several species of tiny squirrels no larger than mice. The PLAIN PIGMY SQUIRREL (*Exilisciurus exilis*) is one of these. Its length is 60 to 80 mm and it is reddish-brown, grey below. An allied species, *E. whiteheadi,* is distinguished by long tufts of hair on its ears.

BLACK GIANT SQUIRREL *(Ratufa bicolor)* Plate 7C
KERAWAK HITAM

Length 330–375 mm, tail 425–460 mm. From the smallest squirrels we now pass abruptly to some of the largest ones, animals as big as rabbits with tails longer than the head and body. This species is black above with pale cheeks and buff or orange below. The voice is a loud bubbling chatter or a quieter double chuckle. It extends from continental Asia into Malaya and the Sunda Islands, except Borneo.

Another species, the CREAM-COLOURED GIANT SQUIRREL (*Ratufa affinis*), KERAWAK PUTIH-KUNING, is found in Thailand, Malaya, Sumatra and Borneo. It has the upperparts cream coloured to light brown with the thighs and shoulders distinctly paler in darker coloured animals.

PLATE 7. A. B. Red Giant Flying Squirrel; C. Black Giant Squirrel; D. Prevost's Squirrel.

PLATE 8. A. Long-tailed Giant Rat; B. House Rat; C. Shrew-faced Ground Squirrel.

PLATE 9. A. Large Bamboo Rat; B. Malayan Pangolin; C. Malayan Porcupine.

PLATE 10. A. Clouded Leopard; B. Dhole; C. Malayan Sun Bear.

The giant squirrels live in the jungle canopy, the tree tops of the high forest. They climb and jump with wonderful activity and when feeding they sit across a large branch with the tail hanging down on one side, balancing the head and fore body on the other. They often associate in pairs or small family groups. Food and breeding habits are as in other arboreal squirrels.

THREE-STRIPED GROUND SQUIRREL *(Lariscus insignis)*   Fig. 8
TUPAI BELANG TIGA
Length 155–190 mm, tail around half body length. Brown above with three black stripes running from the shoulders to the tail, belly pale buff. With this species we leave the squirrels that climb in the trees and introduce the ground squirrels, which pass their lives on

Fig. 8. Three-striped Ground Squirrel.

the forest floor. This is a Sundaland animal, found in the three Sunda Islands and Malaya but not on the Asian mainland. It is a vegetable feeder, not uncommon in forest, and such a confirmed ground dweller that it will seek refuge in a hole or burrow.

SHREW-FACED GROUND SQUIRREL *(Rhinosciurus laticaudatus)*
Plate 8C

TUPAI NANING

Length 185–230 mm, tail 100–150 mm. Head and upperparts brown, underparts dull white, tail short and bushy, snout long and pointed. Not a very common animal, but of interest because it is an example of a squirrel that is adapted to feed on insects. The long snout, very reduced incisor teeth and long tongue are features of this adaptation, and it is known to feed on insects and earthworms. This another Sundaland animal found in Malaya, Borneo and Sumatra.

FLYING SQUIRRELS

These form a distinct group of squirrels which have the power of gliding, just like the colugo, by spreading out a membrane of skin between their fore and hind limbs. Its spread is increased in front by a spur of bone, like an extra finger, that juts out from the wrist. In the giant flying squirrels the membrane is continued across the the base of the tail, which is evenly covered with hair all round. The smaller kinds have no membrane behind the hind limbs and the tail has hairs only on each side, so that it resembles a feather. Flying squirrels are nocturnal, but some of them start activity at dusk and so can sometimes be seen by daylight. They shelter by day in holes in trees and branches or crevices in cliffs.

RED GIANT FLYING SQUIRREL *(Petaurista petaurista)* Plate 7A, B

TUPAI TERBANG MERAH

Length 38–46 cm, tail about the same or a little longer. This is the largest of the Malaysian squirrels, as big as a small cat, with a very long tail. It is dark reddish-brown above, including the flying membrane, paler below, with black tips to the ears, nose, feet and tail.

These squirrels live together in pairs, sometimes accompanied by one or more young ones. They nest in holes in tall trees or in cliffs. In flight they are buoyant and have been observed gliding 400 metres or more when coming down from hills to feed in the forest below.

There are three other species of these very large flying squirrels. The SPOTTED GIANT FLYING SQUIRREL *(Petaurista elegans)* is distinguished from the red giant by having the back spotted with white. The LARGE BLACK FLYING SQUIRREL *(Aeromys tephromelas)* is dark brown or black above, slightly paler below. All three species already mentioned are found in Malaya and Borneo; a fourth, *Aeromys thomasi*, plain brown in colour, is confined to Borneo.

RED-CHEEKED FLYING SQUIRREL *(Hylopetes spadiceus)*   Plate 6A

TUPAI TERBANG PIPI MERAH

Length 135–165 mm, tail 100–140 mm. Dark brown above including tail, cheeks and underparts white with a reddish tinge. This is one of the commoner of the small 'feather-tailed' flying squirrels and is widespread in south-eastern Asia, including Malaya and all the large islands of Sundaland.

HORSFIELD'S FLYING SQUIRREL *(Iomys horsfieldii)*

TUPAI TERBANG EKOR MERAH

Length 175–195 mm tail 160–180 mm. Larger than most of the other small flying squirrels and distinguished by the upper surface of the ear-lobe being hairless. Dark brown above, tail paler and reddish; white below. Widespread in Malaya and Borneo and the rest of Sundaland, and seen in plantations as well as forest. The small flying squirrels are seldom active before dark and must be looked for with a powerful spotlight directed up into the trees.

RATS AND MICE

All over the world a few species of rats and mice have invaded human dwellings, food stores and places of work and are regarded with dislike because they carry disease and do a great deal of damage, and people tend to think of rats and mice in terms of these alone. They are present in Malaysia, but there are many other kinds as well whose home is in forest and open country. They are only a little less diversified than the squirrels, but are much less familiar because they hide by day and are active at night. Rats and mice are also less easy to identify than squirrels because their fur does not have distinctive colour patterns; in the dark these would serve no purpose as marks of recognition. Most of them live on the ground, perhaps because climbing is not easy in darkness but there are some that climb in the trees. They are prolific creatures and may have as many as ten young at a time; the average is five or six.

We will look first at the so-called commensal species, those that live closely associated with man. All the Malaysian species of these are found in Malaya and Borneo.

HOUSE RAT *(Rattus rattus)* Plate 8B

TIKUS RUMAH

Length varying around 150 mm, tail about 100 mm. Olive-brown above, the same or greyish brown below, tail entirely dark brown. The hind foot, from 'heel' to toe is less than 40 mm long. This rat is found all over the world, mainly in towns, and is perhaps the most harmful and dangerous of all mammals. It destroys great quantities of stored food and is a carrier of several diseases of man. The most serious of these is bubonic plague, which is transmitted to man by fleas which leave rats that have died of plague and bite humans, conveying the bacillus of the plague in the act of doing so. Plague epidemics occur in conditions of unhygenic living where rats freely enter dwellings.

NORWAY RAT *(Rattus norvegicus)*

TIKUS MONDOK

Length 160–260 mm, tail 170–230 mm, hind foot of adults over 40 mm long. The fur is brown above, greyish below, the tail dark brown above, pale coloured beneath. The hind foot measurement and tail coloration are the best characters to distinguish the house rat from the Norway rat. It has no particular association with Norway but probably originated on the steppes of central Asia. It is now worldwide in and near human dwellings and in cold climates is the dominant commensal rat. In Malaysia it is restricted to coastal towns.

POLYNESIAN OR LITTLE RAT *(Rattus exulans)*

TIKUS KECIL

Length 100–135 mm, tail a little longer. Dark grey-brown above, dull grey below, tail wholly dark. Smaller size and relatively longer tail distinguish it from the house rat. It lives in cultivated land, often entering houses, and was carried to some of the Pacific islands, including New Zealand, by the early Polynesians in their ocean-going canoes. Its origin is probably somewhere in south-eastern Asia.

The HOUSE MOUSE *(Mus musculus)* is a sort of miniature counterpart of the Norway rat, having a world-wide distribution in towns and also probably originating in the Central Asian grasslands. Its body length is around 75 mm and not over 90 and it is greyish brown, slightly paler below. In Malaysia it is confined to houses in towns. It is the species from which all the variously coloured pet and laboratory mice have been bred.

MALAYSIAN FIELD RAT OR WOOD RAT *(Rattus tiomanicus)*

TIKUS BELUKAR

RICEFIELD RAT *(Rattus argentiventer)*

TIKUS SAWAH

These two species are similar to the house rat and were formerly regarded as subspecies of *Rattus rattus*. Both seem to be confined to Sundaland and they live on the fringes of human habitation. The field rat inhabits secondary forest growth (belukar), gardens, plantations and mangrove. In areas away from the large towns, where the house rat is absent, it enters houses. It is distinguished from the house rat by its white underparts.

The ricefield rat is a little larger on average than the house and field rat and its underparts are silvery grey, often with a dark streak along the midline. It inhabits grassland and ricefields and may be a pest of young oil palms. It does not come into houses.

Of the truly 'wild' rats that live in forest we have space to mention only a selection of the rather numerous species.

Mueller's Rat *(Rattus muelleri)*

TIKUS LEMBAH

About as big as the Norway rat, but the tail is longer, up to 300 mm. Brown above, the fur rather rough textured, white or buff below, tail uniformly dark. This is the common rat of the forest lowlands and swampy areas of Burma, Thailand and Sundaland, except Java. For breeding it makes nests at or a little above ground level.

Long-tailed Giant Rat *(Rattus sabanus)* Plate 8A

TIKUS MONDOK EKOR PANJANG

Length 180–250 mm, tail 270–415 mm. A big rat with a tail up to $1\frac{3}{4}$ times the length of the body. The upperparts are brown grading to chestnut on the head and flanks, the underparts white. Tail dark at the base, pale towards the tip and tending to be darker above than below; the dark and light parts grade together irregularly. Distribution similar to that of Mueller's rat but including Java. It takes the place of that species in the drier parts of the lowland forest on the slopes and ridges between valleys and breeds in shallow burrows in hillsides.

Bower's Rat *(Rattus bowersi)* is another 'giant' rat with a body length of 210–285 mm. It is brown above, whitish below, the tail dark for most of its length but pale towards the tip. It ranges into Malaya from the north and is commonest in the hills; it does not extend into the Sunda Islands. Its chief peculiarity is its surprising tameness; even when trapped these rats are docile and can usually be handled as soon as they are released from the trap.

Brown Spiny Rat or Rajah Rat *(Rattus rajah)*

TIKUS DURI HITAM-PUDAR

Length around 200 mm, tail about the same. Fur brown above, the eye surrounded by grey hairs, white below often with a dark streak in the midline. In this and the other spiny rats there are numerous sharp flattened spines, hidden in the fur but painfully apparent when the animal is handled. The tail is dark above, pale below, with a sharp line of demarcation.

The RED SPINY RAT *(Rattus surifer)* is similar but usually has a chestnut patch on the throat and lacks the mid-ventral dark streak. Both species are found in south-eastern Asia and all over Sundaland and are common in lowland forest. They live and breed in burrows.

Pencil-tailed Tree-mouse *(Chiropodomys glirioides)*

TIKUS BULUH

Length 75–105 mm, tail 100–175 mm. Greyish brown to pale chestnut above, white below, tail dark with longer hairs at the tip. Widely distributed from northern India and southern China to Sundaland. This little climbing rodent is quite common especially where bamboo is growing. It gnaws a circular hole $2\frac{1}{2}$ cm in diameter in a large bamboo and makes a nest of leaves inside; sometimes nests are made in hollow branches of trees. It thrives and will breed in captivity but is very aggressive: even captive-born tree-mice do not become tame.

In Borneo there are two other species of pencil-tailed tree-mice as well as this one, and the island is also the home of the tiny RANEE MICE *(Haeromys,* two species), also tree dwellers.

Large Bamboo Rat *(Rhizomys sumatrensis)*   Plate 9A

DEKAN

Length 260–380 mm, tail half the length or less. The bamboo rats are classified separately from the rest of the rats and mice (Muridae) in a family of their own, the Rhizomidae. The most obvious difference is in the tail, which is smooth and hairless in the bamboo rats and is covered with scales and short bristles in the Muridae. The large bamboo rat has short coarse brownish grey fur and is a thickset animal with strong claws and very large broad incisor teeth which are exposed in a threatening display when the animal is frightened. They are not uncommon and live in burrows under large bamboo clumps, which are dug with the powerful claws and teeth. Their natural food is bamboo roots but they will eat tapioca and sugar cane roots in plantations. They become tame in captivity and thrive on a diet of sweet potato, fruit and fresh bones, the latter being necessary to keep them in good health.

This and another rather smaller species, the HOARY BAMBOO RAT *(Rhizomys pruinosus)* range into Malaya from the Asian continent and are not found in Borneo. The larger species lives all over Malaya, the other which is chocolate brown with the hairs white-tipped, is confined to the northern States.

PORCUPINES

The largest of the Asian rodents are the porcupines, of which four species are found in Malaysia, all rather localised in their distribution. A fifth lives in Java and is confined to that island. All of them are protected by a coat of hard sharp spines which grow among the fur and are themselves modified hairs. The larger kinds, both in Malaysia and elswhere in Asia and Africa, are so well protected that they have little fear of predators; even tigers cannot attack them successfully. They generally stand their ground and raise the conspicuous armament of spines in a warning display, at the same time vibrating the tail to make a rattling or buzzing sound. If actually molested a porcupine turns and runs backwards at its enemy's face and front paws. Any spines that are implanted are easily pulled out at their bases and remain to work into the victim's flesh and give rise to suppurating crippling wounds. The Asian porcupines are ground-living animals and dig burrows in which they rest by day and have their young. In the species whose breeding has been observed one young is born, rarely two.

MALAYAN PORCUPINE *(Hystrix brachyura)* Plate 9C

LANDAK RAYA, LANDAK TUNGGAL

Length about 70 cm and weight up to 8 kg (17 or 18 pounds). This is the largest Malaysian species and is confined to southern Thailand, Malaya, Sumatra and Borneo. The spines are long, black-and-white and round in cross section. It habits are as described for the larger porcupines and it feeds mainly on roots, tubers and fallen fruit. It also has a keen appetite for bones and teeth well capable of dealing with them. If an elephant dies in the jungle its skeleton is soon demolished by porcupines: even the ivory of the tusks is gnawed away, presumably to get at the central pulp. In captivity they should be given fresh bones in addition to vegetable food.

THICK-SPINED PORCUPINE *(Thecurus crassispinis)*

LANDAK BORNEO

Length between 50–60 cm. The spines are brown-and-white and have a groove along one side. This species is confined to Borneo and Sumatra and seems to be more common in Borneo than the Malayan porcupine. The two species have similar habits.

BRUSH-TAILED PORCUPINE *(Atherurus macrourus)* Fig. 9

Fig. 9. Brush-tailed Porcupine.

LANDAK BATU, LANDAK NIBONG, LANDAK KELUBI
Length 38–50 cm, tail 10–20 cm. Brown above with many flattened spines and some round pale-coloured ones. The end of the tail has a cluster of long whitish hairs modified in such a way that they look like strings of flattened beads. The spines of the back are quite long but much less conspicuous than those of the large porcupines. Distribution, southern Thailand, Malaya and Sumatra, not Borneo. This animal is not often seen but is fairly common in forest.

LONG-TAILED PORCUPINE *(Trichys lipura)* Fig. 10
LANDAK PADI
Length about 40 cm, tail half as long or a little more. The spines are short and flattened and hardly project beyond the hair, so that the animal looks rather like an enormous rat. The tail ends in a tuft of large flattened hairs. This species is found in Malaya, Borneo and Sumatra but does not seem to be common anywhere.

Fig. 10. Long-tailed Porcupine.

CARNIVORA

The name of this Order means 'flesh-eaters' and most of the mammals belonging to it are adapted for hunting prey as large as, or not much smaller than, themselves, and feeding on flesh. They are all strong, active animals, but the most characteristic features associated with killing and meat eating are seen in their teeth. The canine teeth are almost always long and sharp and used as weapons for killing prey and for fighting. In the upper jaw the last premolars, and in the lower jaw the first molars, are specially adapted for cutting through flesh with a scissor-like action. These four teeth are known as the carnassial teeth and are only developed in this way in the Carnivora. Meat is easily digested and can be swallowed in lumps without mastication. Although mainly meat eaters the mammals of this Order do take vegetable food; some of them, particularly the bears, live on a very mixed diet and their teeth are blunt and effective in mashing up rather than slicing it. The Carnivora range very widely in size from large formidable animals like tigers and bears down to weasels no larger than rats or mice.

The dogs and bears are represented in Malaysia by one species each, the cats and the mustelids or weasels by several species and the civets and mongooses by no less than eighteen.

RED DOG OR DHOLE *(Cuon alpinus)*   Plate 10B
SERIGALA

Length up to one metre, tail less than half head and body. Distributed in central and eastern Asia, Malaya, Sumatra Java but not Borneo. The dhole is not one of the true dogs (*Canis*) but is placed in a genus *Cuon* on its own. It is reddish or chestnut above, paler below, with a black bushy tail, and is distinguished from domestic dogs that have run wild by the colour, the short rounded ears and thick hair between the pads of the feet. Also the lower jaw has only six teeth behind the canine; dogs have seven.

Dhole hunt in small packs of five or six or a few more and by cooperating in the kill can pull down animals as large as sambar or wild pig. A large territory is needed to provide food for a pack and, perhaps for this reason, they are never common. Litters range from 2 to 7 puppies.

Malayan Sun Bear *(Helarctos malayanus)* Plate 10C

BERUANG

Length from one to nearly 1½ metres, tail very short, the smallest of all the bears. Found from north-eastern India to Malaya and the Sunda Islands except Java, living in lowland and mountain forest. The colour is almost black and there is a white or yellowish mark on the chest, often but not always V-shaped. Each foot bears five large claws.

The Sun Bear is mainly nocturnal and climbs well, leaving characteristic claw marks on the trunks of trees. It feeds on fruits and other vegetation, termites, wild honey when it can get it, and it probably catches and eats small vertebrates as well. One or two cubs are born at a time. This is a dangerous animal if accidentally approached by day in its den under a log or between the buttress roots of a large tree. It tends to attack rather than run away, females with young being specially aggressive, and its powerful teeth and claws can inflict terrible wounds.

Young sun bears are attractive little animals and soon become tame and apparently domesticated, but when they approach full size they are most unsafe pets. It is better not to keep and become fond of a sun bear.

CATS

The cats are the most highly developed of the Carnivora and are almost exclusively carnivorous in their diet. They are specialised for hunting and killing and most of them are nocturnal. Nearly all except the largest are expert climbers and this has led to their sense of sight becoming predominant over that of smell. The muzzle is foreshortened to form a 'face' and the eyes directed forwards, giving the binocular vision needed for judging distance. They also have exceptionally good night vision accompanied by a vertical pupil which is dilated in the dark and narrowed to a slit to protect the eye from the strong light of day. With one exception, the cheetah, not, of course, found in Malaya, the claws are fully retractile, that is they can be withdrawn into sheaths so that they are not blunted by contact with the ground but kept sharp for climbing and for use as weapons. When a cat 'sharpens' its claws on the furniture it is not, of course, sharpening them at all, but stretching or exercising the muscles that control them. Wild cats of all kinds perform this exercise on tree trunks and branches. The teeth are specialised for flesh eating, the canines and carnassials being large and the number of cheek teeth reduced to three or four in the upper jaw and three in the lower.

There are eight species of cats in Malaysia of which three are not found in Borneo and one is confined to that island. We will start with the largest of them.

TIGER *(Panthera tigris)*   Plate 11C
HARIMAU BELANG

Recorded measurements of tigers usually include the tail, and the average total length of Malayan tigers is 2.5 to 2.75 metres (8 to 9 feet, the tail being between 1/2 and 2/3 of the head and body; weight up to 225 kg or nearly 500 pounds. The geographical range is from the tropics of Asia to northern China and Siberia and formerly to western Iran, where it is now extinct. Tigers occur, (or did until recently), in Malaya, Java and Sumatra but not in Borneo. Those of cold climates are the biggest and a Siberian tiger of nearly 4 metres (13 feet) has been recorded, Their numbers in the wild are now dwindling rapidly over the whole of their range.

Tigers are solitary animals apart from the temporary bond between the mother and cubs, which number from one to four in a litter. Their main prey in Malaya is wild pig, but they will eat small animals, even frogs and fish, when hungry. Domestic animals such as goats and young buffaloes are readily taken. They do not often attack humans but it cannot be said that they never do so.

A world without any wild tigers at all would be a sadly diminished place, but to people living in villages in the country tigers are not good neighbours; they are sometimes dangerous and always alarming to meet and they take their toll of valuable domestic beasts. In the modern world their existence is only acceptable in places set apart for them and not settled by any human population, which is to say in nature reserves. These must be of large extent and must be protected by law against any sort of development, whether hunting, settlement, timber-felling or mining, and the law must be backed by public sentiment; if not it will be ineffectual.

Leopard or Panther *(Panthera pardus)* Plate 11A, B

HARIMAU BINTANG
HARIMAU KUMBANG (black panther)

Average length of males, with tail, 2.1 metres (7 feet), females rather less. A very widespread animal ranging over most of Africa and Asia including Malaya: on the Sunda Islands only in Java. There are two colour forms, one pale tawny with numerous black rosettes, the other also marked with black rosettes but with the ground colour so dark that they are hardly visible. When a 'black panther' skin fades from long exposure to the light the spots show up clearly. The black form is associated with rain forest and in Malaya by far outnumbers the normal spotted one. Black and spotted kittens may appear in the same litter and there is no difference in temperament, or any feature other than colour, between the two.

Leopards climb well and prey on monkeys, mouse-deer, wild pig and ground-living birds; they are also partial to domestic dogs. They are dangerous if approached when wounded. The voice is a regularly repeated coughing roar said to resemble the sound of sawing wood. One to three kittens are the usual litter. Like tigers, leopards are decreasing in numbers everywhere, both from destruction of their habitat and from hunting in order to sell the skins, which are still in demand for feminine adornment in spite of propaganda against wearing them.

Clouded Leopard *(Neofelis nebulosa)* Plate 10A

HARIMAU DAHAN

Head and body up to one metre, tail nearly as long and thickly furred. The canine teeth are long and blade-like. Colour and pattern as illustrated: this is one of the most beautifully marked of all the cats. Its home is in the forests of eastern Asia, Malaya, Sumatra and Borneo.

In size it is between the 'great cats' (tiger and panther) and the small ones and it is largely arboreal, spending more time in the trees than on the ground. Its hunting habits are similar to those of the leopard but with the emphasis on smaller game. It has no reputation of being dangerous to man. Clouded leopards are nowhere common and are more strictly confined to forest than the tiger and panther.

Leopard Cat *(Felis bengalensis)*   Plate 12C

KUCING BATU

Length 45–55 cm, tail less than half length. Widespread from India and the Himalayas to eastern Asia, the Sunda Islands and the Philippines, inhabiting a wide climatic range. Its colour is tawny with a conspicuous pattern of round black spots which tend to be elongate on the fore legs and shoulders; face vertically striped; back of the ear black with a white spot.

This is the only one of the small cats that is at all common in Malaysia. It inhabits all kinds of country, forest, plantations and even suburban areas, and is notorious as a chicken thief. Its natural prey consists of small mammals and birds, lizards and frogs. It mews harshly and purrs when pleased but is difficult to tame; kittens taken very young sometimes become docile.

The other four Malaysian small cats are all rare. Two are found in both Malaya and Borneo, the MARBLED CAT *(Felis marmorata)* and the FLAT-HEADED CAT *(Felis planiceps)*. The former has a pattern rather like that of a clouded leopard, but is of course much smaller. The tail is as long as the head and body, a feature that immediately distinguishes it from the leopard cat. It is found in the warmer parts of Asia eastwards from the Himalayas. The flat-headed cat has a more restricted range from southern Thailand and Malaya to Sumatra and Borneo. It is dark or greyish-brown above, paler below, with a speckled or grizzled appearance. The fur is short and the tail very short, a little over a quarter of the body length. The kittens are grey.

The GOLDEN CAT *(Felis temminckii)* is a little larger than the others and is a beautiful animal, plain golden brown all over except for the face which has an elegant pattern of dark and white stripes. It ranges from the mainland into Malaya and Sumatra. In Borneo, and confined to the island, lives the BAY CAT *(Felis badia)* which is plain yellowish brown or chestnut without any spots or stripes, the only marking being a white patch on the underside of the tail. It is a rare forest animal about which little is known.

CIVETS AND MONGOOSES

The civets resemble the small cats in size and in having patterns of spots or stripes on head, body and tail, but the muzzle is always pointed. They are not closely related to cats and are in fact rather primitive members of the Carnivora. Most of them have well developed scent glands near the anus, and the secretion produced in this way by members of the genus *Viverra* is used in making perfume. Some of them are by no means strict carnivores but vary a flesh diet with fruit. Many of them are good climbers and these generally have partially retractile claws, and they are all normally nocturnal. Most of the civets are easily tamed.

The mongooses are classified with the civets in the family Viverridae, but have a rather different appearance. They are plain coloured, short-legged ground dwellers and are very efficient predators on small mammals and reptiles and on birds and their eggs. In general mongooses inhabit more open country than the forest-loving true civets. As could be expected the latter are well represented in Malaysia, the mongooses less so. The following account includes all but a few rare and obscure species.

MALAY CIVET *(Viverra tangalunga)* Fig. 11
TENGGALUNG

Length around 65 cm, tail about half length. This is a Sundaland animal, inhabiting Malaya, Borneo and Sumatra but not Java. It is tawny grey striped with black and has the throat conspicuously patterned black and white. The tail is marked with about ten black and white rings and the black rings are joined on the top of the basal half of the tail by a black stripe continuous with a central dorsal stripe on the body. This tail pattern distinguishes this from the other similar species found in Malaysia. The Malay civet is a ground-dwelling animal, not uncommon and a predator of small animals including reptiles and insects.

In addition to this one three allied species are found in Malaya and on the continent to the north, but not in Borneo. They all have the conspicuous dark and pale patterned throat and are distinguished from the Malay civet as follows:

LARGE INDIAN CIVET *(Viverra zibetha)*, larger, up to 80 cm, tail with five or six completely separated dark and pale rings, only the basal dark ring joined to the dorsal stripe; indistinct dark spots on the flanks.

PLATE 11. A. B. Panther, black and spotted varieties; C. Tiger.

PLATE 12. A. Small-clawed Otter; B. Yellow-throated Marten; C. Leopard Cat.

PLATE 13. A. Masked Palm Civet; B. Common Palm Civet; C. Binturong.

PLATE 14. A. Sumatran Rhinoceros; B. Gaur; C. Indian Elephant

Fig. 11. Malay Civet.

LARGE SPOTTED CIVET *(Viverra megaspila)*, length up to 95 cm, basal half of tail with three or four dark rings joined together on top and with the dorsal stripe, terminal half dark with indistinct paler rings; large irregular dark spots on the flanks.

LITTLE CIVET *(Viverricula malaccensis)*, smaller, tail marked with seven complete dark rings, its tip usually pale; flanks with numerous dark spots arranged in rows. All three, like the Malay civet, are ground-living animals.

COMMON PALM CIVET OR TODDY CAT *(Paradoxurus hermaphroditus)*
Plate 13B

MUSANG PULUT

Length 50–60 cm, tail about the same. Ranges from India and Ceylon through Sundaland to the Philippines, Celebes and the Lesser Sunda Islands. The colour varies from dark to pale grey and there are three distinct parallel dark lines along the back and black spots on the flanks. There is a dark patch on each side of the face, enclosing the eyes, throat uniform grey, tail not ringed.

This is the common musang that lives in forest, plantations and settled areas and often finds its way into roof spaces of houses; it is naturally an arboreal animal. It combines a flesh and fruit diet and is fond of drinking from the vessels put in palm trees to collect sap for making toddy or palm sugar. There are usually three young, born in a hollow tree or a space among rocks.

MASKED PALM CIVET *(Paguma larvata)*   Plate 13A

MUSANG LAMRI
Length 60–70 cm, tail the same. Ranges from the continent into Malaya, Sumatra and Borneo. The colour is plain reddish brown without spots or stripes and the face is marked with a pattern of dark stripes and pale patches which may extend back to the nape. This civet is found in all types of forest. It lives largely on figs and other fruits and has been caught taking tomatoes from a garden; no doubt it takes animal food as well.

SMALL-TOOTHED OR THREE-STRIPED PALM CIVET *(Arctogalidia trivirgata)*

MUSANG AKAR
Length around 55 cm, tail a little longer. Found in continental Asia and the whole of Sundaland. The colour is dark to light grey and there are three narrow black lines along the back, but the flanks, unlike those of the toddy cat, are unmarked. The tail is to some degree prehensile and used in climbing. This civet lives in forest but has been reported as eating young pods on cocoa plantations in Malaya. Its normal diet appears to be mixed like that of other civets.

BINTURONG OR BEARCAT *(Arctitis binturong)*   Plate 13C

BINTURUNG
Length 60 to over 95 cm tail a little shorter, the largest of all the Malaysian civets. Found in south-eastern Asia through the Sunda Islands to the Philippines. The fur is shaggy and almost black and there are tufts of hair on the ears. The binturong lives in forest and climbs well, and it can hang by its tail which is fully prehensile. It eats fruit and also catches reptiles and other small animals.

Three rather rare civets remain to be mentioned. The BANDED LINSANG *(Prionodon linsang)* is a beautiful animal, smaller than other

Fig. 12. Banded Linsang.

Fig. 13. Banded Palm Civet.

civets and with fully retractile claws. It is marked with a pattern of pale yellow and black bars and spots over the back and on the neck and flanks; the tail is long and banded black and yellow for the whole of its length. The BANDED PALM CIVET *(Hemigalus derbyanus)* is pale buff with a pattern of black bars over the back and narrow black stripes on the top of the head. The flanks and legs are not marked with black and the terminal two-thirds of the tail is uniformly dark. Both are uncommon animals of lowland forest, the banded linsang the rarer of the two. The OTTER CIVET *(Cynogale bennettii)* is aquatic and has come by convergent evolution to resemble an otter. It has a short tail and long stiff whiskers and hunts fish and frogs in the water. These three species are found in Malaya and Borneo.

SHORT-TAILED MONGOOSE *(Herpestes brachyurus)*

BAMBUN EKOR PENDEK

Length up to 47 cm, tail about half length. Confined to Malaya, Sumatra and Borneo, this is the only mongoose with a Sundaland distribution. The lack of markings on both head and body distinguish the mongooses from the civets. The black and brown banded hairs

Fig. 14. Short-tailed Mongoose.

give this species an appearance of being brown finely speckled with black. Like all the mongooses it is carnivorous and egg-eating, and when angry or frightened it erects the hairs on the back and tail.

Two other mongooses are recorded from Borneo; of one of them HOSE'S MONGOOSE *(Herpestes hosei)*, only one specimen is known. Three others, not found in Borneo, are on the Malayan list ,but two of these are Indian species which may have been artificially introduced. The third is the JAVAN MONGOOSE *(Herpestes javanicus)*, which is also found in south-eastern Asia and Java. It is distinguished by a suffusion of reddish brown on the head, back and tail.

MUSTELIDAE: WEASELS, OTTERS, BADGERS

The mustelids include the smallest of all the Carnivora and none of them are large animals. They are more characteristic of the cool and cold parts of Asia, Europe and North America than of the tropics, and are typically short-legged long-bodied beasts. Many of them have anal glands producing a strong-smelling secretion which may be so repugnant that it serves as a means of defence, as in the American skunks. The claws are never retractile and most mustelids are ground dwellers or aquatic. The majority are strictly carnivorous.

In Malaysia the small weasel-like mustelids are poorly represented by only two species, but there are three, possibly four, species of otter. Two badger-like animals are found, but both are confined to Borneo and one or more of the other Sunda Islands and do not extend to Malaya.

YELLOW-THROATED MARTEN *(Martes flavigula)* Plate 12B

MENGKIRA

Length 45–50 cm, tail 40 cm. Found in eastern Asia from Siberia south to Malaya and the Sunda Islands including Borneo. It is brown with the throat and chest conspicuously yellow or orange; the tail is rather thickly furred.

The martens, including this one, form an exception among the mustelids in being largely arboreal. Although it is often active by day it is seldom seen and seems not to be common anywhere. It preys on birds and their eggs, small mammals and reptiles and is said to eat fruit as well.

Malay Weasel *(Mustela nudipes)*

PULASAN

Length 300–350 mm, tail more than half length. A Sundaland animal found in Malaya, Sumatra and Borneo. Body pale yellowish brown, the head nearly white. A typical weasel with long body, very short legs and a strong acrid smell. It is a ground dweller and strictly carnivorous but little seems to be known about its habits.

Small-clawed Otter *(Amblonyx cinerea)*   Plate 12A

BERANG-BERANG

Length 42–54 cm, tail 23–33 cm. Found in India and eastern Asia to the Sunda Islands and the Philippines. Slatey grey or brown above, slightly paler below. Very small ears and long stiff whiskers are characteristic of the otters, and a tail more than half the length of the head and body distinguish them from the otter civet. This is a small otter and its claws are rudimentary, not projecting beyond the tips of the fingers and toes. It is often active by day and seen on the banks of rivers, sometimes in small family parties. It feeds on fish, frogs, crabs and water snails. The fore feet are used for finding and catching prey and are very 'clever' at manipulation; pet small-clawed otters constantly juggle and play with small objects.

The HAIRY-NOSED OTTER *(Lutra sumatrana)* is also found in both Malaya and Borneo. It is much larger than the small-clawed (length about 80 cm) and has fully webbed feet and well developed claws, and is not nearly so clever with its 'hands'. It lives in large rivers, often near their mouths, and even in the sea.

In Malaya, but not Borneo, another medium-sized otter is fairly common in the large rivers. This is the SMOOTH OTTER *(Lutra perspicillata)* which has sleek, smooth fur. Its nose is hairless, a feature which readily distinguishes it from *Lutra sumatrana*. One specimen of the widely distributed COMMON OTTER *(Lutra lutra)* has been recorded from the Langkawi Islands off north-western Malaya.

Javanese Ferret-Badger *(Melogale orientalis)*

PULASAN LAMRI

Length 30–35 cm, tail less than half length. Confined to Java and

Borneo, where it is known from the slopes of Mount Kinabalu. It is dull brown with a bushy tail and white or pale buff markings on the face and nape of the neck and whitish ears. As its name implies it is more slender and ferret- or weasel-like than the typical badgers, but it has strong digging claws which is a badger characteristic.

TELEDU OR MALAYSIAN STINK BADGER *(Mydaus javanensis)*

TELEDU

Length 35–55 cm, tail very short. This is another Sundaland mammal found in Borneo, Sumatra and Java. It is a typical small badger, black all over except for a white crown on the head and a white stripe down the middle of the back. It is probable that this is a pattern of warning colours, as the smell of this animal is said to be appalling. In the past, when collections of Malaysian mammals were being made for museums, hardened animal collectors, given the job of skinning and preparing a teledu, were usually sick before they could finish. As far as is known it feeds on insects and other small animals and lives in burrows, which are said sometimes to be shared with porcupines.

THE LARGE HERBIVORES

This is a convenient heading under which to group the remainder of the Malaysian land mammals. They are included in three Orders, the PROBOSCIDEA or elephants, the PERISSODACTYLA or odd-toed hoofed mammals, and the ARTIODACTYLA or even-toed hoofed mammals. Most of them are large animals and the only small ones, the mouse-deer, are exceptionally small members of their Order.

The two existing species of elephant, living in Africa and Asia respectively, are a last remnant of a once diverse assemblage of huge mammals with trunks and tusks developed in various ways. At least two of these, the mammoth in Eurasia and the mastodon in America, survived into the times of stone-age man, who probably played a part in exterminating them.

The perissodactyls and artiodactyls are the hoofed mammals, formerly classified together as 'ungulates', but now known to have wholly separate evolutionary origins. All of them stand permanently on the tips of their toes, an adaptation for fast running. The 'knee' of a horse is really its wrist and the 'hock' is its heel. There has been an accompanying reduction in the number of the digits, to four, three or one in the perissodactyls, or to two, the equally developed third and fourth fingers and toes, in the artiodactyls. The hoofs are, of course, simply modified claws or nails. Vestiges of the reduced digits are present in the form of 'splint bones' and in the very primitive tapirs the fore foot has four toes that reach the ground.

In Malaysia, the perissodactyls are represented by the tapir and rhinoceros, both of which are relations of the horse in which reduction of the digits is still in its early stages, far short of the single fingers and toes on which a horse stands and runs. The artiodactyls are the pigs, cattle, goats, deer and mouse-deer. In these the axis of both fore and hind foot runs between the third and fourth digits so that two is the limit to which they can be reduced. With the exception of the wild pigs all the Malaysian artiodactyls are ruminants. That is to say they have the stomach divided into compartments and chew their food over again after swallowing it for the first time. This is an adaptation for extracting as much nourishment as possible from indigestible vegetable food.

Most of the Malaysian ungulates feel the need to add salt to their diet and eagerly visit mineral springs or 'salt-licks' to drink the water or, more usually, to eat the earth surrounding them. Good game wardens add crude salt to the salt licks in their territory, and there is no doubt that the animals welcome it.

PROBOSCIDEA
ELEPHANTS

INDIAN ELEPHANT *(Elephas maximus)* Plate 14C

GAJAH

The elephant requires no description. The Asian species, in spite of its Latin name, is smaller than the African; a large Indian elephant weighs between 3 and 4 tons. They are found as wild animals in India, south-eastern Asia, Malaya, Sumatra and Borneo.

In Malaya elephants are undoubtedly indigenous. In Borneo there is, in the north-eastern part of the island, a wild population of them

PLATE 15. A. Bearded Pig; B. Malayan Tapir; C. Sambar.

PLATE 16. A. Large Mouse-deer; B. Barking Deer; Serow.

which is generally supposed to be derived from animals that escaped from domestication by the Brunei sultans; trained elephants were seen in Brunei as early as 1521. On the other hand fossil remains from the Pleistocene Epoch or 'Ice Age' have been found in Borneo and it is possible that they have survived as wild animals there since the time when Sundaland was more or less extensively joined to the mainland of Asia.

Elephants need large quantities of vegetable food, as much as 250 kg or a quarter of a ton, a day. They have no inhibitions about invading standing crops and they do serious damage, as much by trampling as in feeding, but the construction of ditches only 6 to 8 feet wide will prevent the entry of elephants into cultivated land. Nevertheless, like tigers, wild elephants are not good country neighbours; they must be accommodated in large nature reserves if they are to live at all.

Usually one young is born at a time after a gestation period of about 21 months. Maturity is reached after 8 to 12 years and the expectation of life is rather less than that of modern man; an age of 70 is exceptional for an elephant.

The tusks, which are much larger in males, are really enormous foreward-growing incisor teeth. An elephant's life span is limited by the duration of its molar teeth, of which it has the use, in succession, of six in each jaw. They do not grow and erupt together, but one after the other throughout its life, only one enormous molar (or parts of two) being present in the jaw at any one time. As it wears down each one is substituted from behind by the next one in succession, and when the sixth and last molars have erupted and worn away the elephant can no longer chew its food.

PERISSODACTYLA

SUMATRAN RHINOCEROS *(Didermocerus sumatrensis)*   Plate 14A

BADAK BERENDAM

This is the smallest of the five existing species of rhinoceros, 2.5 to 2.8 metres long and a little over a metre in height at the shoulder. It is more hairy than any of the others and has two horns on its snout, the hinder one often very small. There are two folds in the skin, one over the shoulders and one on each side in front of the hind quarters. In colour it appears dark brown or blackish. The footprints are much more likely to be seen than the animal; they are three-toed and around 20 cm in diameter.

Rhinoceroses all over their range in Asia and Africa are threatened with extinction largely due to a superstitious belief that the substance of their horns, and other parts of them, are of medicinal value, especially in promoting virility. There is no foundation for this belief; the horns of rhinos have the same constitution as hair, and scrapings from one have the same therapeutic value, or lack of it, as chopped up horsehair.

There are now a few, very few, Sumatran rhinos left in the hill forests of Malaya, Borneo and Sumatra, and it seems that their numbers are still diminishing. They are, of course, protected by law, but a rational and realistic attitude towards them would be of more value to their survival.

Another species, the JAVAN RHINOCEROS *(Rhinoceros sondaicus)*, existed in Malaya up to the first quarter of this century, the last ones having been shot near Teluk Anson in 1932. It is now known to exist only in a small population in the Hudjong Kulong Reserve in western Java, where it is carefully guarded by the Indonesian Government. The Javan rhino is much larger than the Sumatran, 1.4 to 1.7 metres high at the shoulder, and it has only one horn and three folds of skin running over the back and flanks.

MALAYAN TAPIR *(Tapirus indicus)* Plate 15B

TENUK, CIPAN, BADAK MURAI

Length between 2 and 2.5 metres, a little smaller than the Sumatran rhino. The tracks are also smaller, not more than 17 cm in diameter, and those of the fore foot are four-toed. The distribution is southeastern Asia extending to Malaya and Sumatra, not Borneo. The young tapir is brown with a pattern of irregular yellowish longitudinal stripes; as the animal grows up this is gradually replaced by the remarkable black-and-white coloration of the adult. Both patterns can be regarded as camouflage. A curled up sleeping young tapir looks very much like a heap of sun-dappled dead leaves. The adult pattern may well be a bold essay in what is called disruptive coloration; its effect is to convey an impression of either half a black animal or half a white one. The eye of the tiger is not automatically alerted by an image of half an animal and so fails to spot the tapir so long as it remains motionless. Tapirs are active mainly at night and they do hide effectively by day because they are very seldom seen.

This animal suffers no particular persecution but is growing scarcer as the forest dwindles away. It is a curious and interesting beast, remarkable in appearance and a 'living fossil', a relic of a once widespread and varied fauna of primitive perissodactyls. Their only other modern habitat is tropical Central and South America, where three species are found, all plain coloured as adults but similarly striped when young.

ARTIODACTYLA

Wild Pig *(Sus scrofa)*

BABI HUTAN

About 80 cm high at the shoulder and may weigh well over 100 kg. Brown with black bristles forming a crest over the shoulders and along the back; the young are marked with light and dark longitudinal stripes. The canine teeth of both jaws grow continously and are developed as tusks which are formidable weapons, especially in the male or boar. This is the wild pig or 'wild boar' that extends from Europe to eastern Asia and to the Sunda Islands except Borneo.

Wild pigs are active by day and night and in spite of being constantly hunted they seem to maintain their numbers fairly well. They feed by rooting in the soil and do serious damage to such crops as sweet potato and tapioca. They may be solitary or go in small parties, and several young are born at a time, exceptionally as many as 11, but no litters of this size have been recorded from Malaya.

Bearded Pig *(Sus barbatus)* Plate 15A

BABI BODOH, BABI JOKUT

This animal is larger than the common wild pig and paler coloured with a longer head and a conspicuous growth of bristles around the jaws. It is found in Malaya and Sumatra and is the only wild pig present in Borneo. It seems to be less shy than the smaller species and sometimes congregates in quite large herds which migrate from one district to another. When they are swimming across rivers such herds are very vulnerable to hunting. Their numbers have become depleted in recent years.

TRAGULIDAE, CHEVROTAINS OR MOUSE-DEER

This is a Family of ruminants including only four known species, three Asian and one African. They are not closely related to the true deer and are among the smallest of all hoofed animals.

LESSER MOUSE-DEER *(Tragulus javanicus)*

PELANDUK, KANCIL

Length 40–48 cm, tail short, weight up to 2 kg. or a little more; legs very slender ending in tiny hoofs; reddish brown with an unbroken white stripe running from jaw to shoulder. Found in south-eastern Asia and all the Sunda Islands. The LARGE MOUSE-DEER *(Tragulus napu)*, NAPOH, Plate 16, is bigger, less red in colour and the stripe on the side of the throat is broken or irregular. Its distribution is similar to that of the other species but excludes Java.

Mouse-deer live in forest, both primary and secondary and are nocturnal; the smaller species is the more common but neither is rare. Usually one young is born, sometimes two, and they are active within an hour of birth. In Malay folklore the mouse-deer bears the character of the little fellow who scores off his larger and stronger companions by superior cunning. 'Sang Kanchil' meets the tiger, the crocodiles and other large and fierce members of the fauna and always gets the better of them.

CERVIDAE OR TRUE DEER

These form a very distinct group of ruminants whose characteristic is the growth of antlers on the head, which are usually branched and which fall off periodically and are regrown. In countries with marked seasons they are grown and shed in an annual cycle, but in the two Malaysian species the cycle is irregular. With one exception, the reindeer or caribou of the Arctic region, antlers are grown only by males.

SAMBAR *(Cervus unicolor)* Plate 15C
RUSA

Height at shoulder 1 to nearly $1\frac{1}{2}$ metres. Dark to pale uniform brown, the young or fawns may be faintly spotted at birth. The first antlers grown by a male are simple spikes, the second pair have two points or tines and later antlers have no more than three. The sambar ranges from India to Malaya, all the Sunda Islands and Sulawesi (Celebes).

Sambar live in forest, feeding mainly in clearings and going singly or in small groups. The voice is a high-pitched grunt and they stamp their feet when suspicious of danger. Their meat, known as venison, is very good and they are hunted everywhere where forest is accessible from human habitation.

BARKING DEER OR INDIAN MUNTJAC *(Muntiacus muntjak)*
Plate 16B

KIJANG

This is a small deer, 40–55 cm high at the shoulder. Tawny brown, white on the throat and under the tail. Males have short two-tined antlers on long hair-covered bases or pedicels, and they also have prominent upper canine teeth. The young are spotted until about six months old. Widely distributed from India to southern China and south to Malaya and all the Sunda Islands. Muntjac live in thick forest and are not often seen. The call is a hoarse bark.

BOVIDAE OR HOLLOW-HORNED RUMINANTS

These include cattle, goats and antelopes and are more characteristic of open savannah or mountain country than of thick forest. Only three of them live as native wild animals in Malaysia. There are 'wild' water buffalo in Borneo, but they have most probably originated from escaped domestic animals.

Gaur or Seladang *(Bos gaurus)*   Plate 14B

SELADANG

This is the largest and heaviest of all wild cattle, big bulls stand nearly two metres high at the shoulder. Over and behind the shoulders the back is raised to form a hump-like crest. The body in adult males and females is almost black with the hair on the forehead and between the bases of the horns pale grey, and there are white 'stockings' on the fore and hind legs. Young gaur, up to six months old, are bright golden brown. Gaur range from India through Burma to south-eastern Asia and Malaya, but not to any of the Sunda Islands. The gayal of Burma is possibly a domesticated race of the gaur.

They feed by grazing, not from the leaves of trees and bushes, and therefore need clearings where grass is available. They frequent salt-licks and can be attracted by clearing a wide space of trees and allowing grass to grow, as at Kuala Tahan in the Taman Negara. They are magnificent animals and fully justify the conservation of forest needed to keep them in existence.

Banteng *(Bos javanicus)*

BANTENG, TEMADAU

This is a smaller animal than the gaur and lacks the hump-like crest over the shoulders. Bulls are blackish but cows and young animals are pale brown. They have white 'stockings' and a very distinctive white patch on the hind quarters below the tail; this immediately distinguishes banteng from gaur. The range is from south-eastern Asia southward to Borneo and Java, but in Malaya they have always been confined to the northern States and may now be extinct there. Banteng are domesticated on a large scale in Java and Bali.

Serow *(Capricornis sumatraensis)*   Plate 16C

KAMBING GURUN

Height at shoulder a little less than a metre. A goat-like animal with dark brown hair tinged with grey or red and a heavy mane on the neck. Both sexes have a pair of curved horns. The range is from the Himalayas to south-western China and south to Malaya and Sumatra.

The serow is really a mountain animal and climbs with great agility in rocky country and on cliffs. In Malaya it lives both on steep forested slopes and on the limestone hills in the centre and north of the country. It is not a true goat but is related to the European chamois and the North American Rocky Mountain goat.

This brings us to the end of the mammals that live on land. Of the marine species only one can be said to be Malaysian in any real sense, the coast-living dugong. Whales, porpoises and dolphins may stray into our waters from anywhere in the Pacific and Indian Oceans. I shall describe only a few of them, the species that are most frequently seen.

SIRENIA
DUGONG AND MANATEES

The sirenians or 'sea cows' are curious, entirely aquatic mammals that live in tropical coastal waters. There are three species of manatee, two found on the American Atlantic coast, one on the African. The dugong lives in the Indian and western Pacific Oceans. A fifth sirenian was discovered in the Arctic waters of the Bering Strait rather over 200 years ago and exterminated by hunting only thirty years after its discovery. This was Steller's sea cow, a huge animal ten metres long and weighing about three tons.

Sirenians are rather whale-like in appearance with no external trace of hind limbs and paddle-like fore limbs; the tail is horizontally flattened for swimming, very like a whale's. The females are said to hold their young in their paddles and suckle them at a pair of breasts near the bases of the paddles in a very human-like manner. For this reason, perhaps, they have come to be called Sirenia or 'sirens' and associated with the legendary mermaids. There is certainly nothing in their actual appearance to support this notion. They are entirely herbivorous and their fossil history suggests that they are related to elephants. All the surviving species are all too easy to hunt and kill and are in danger of extinction.

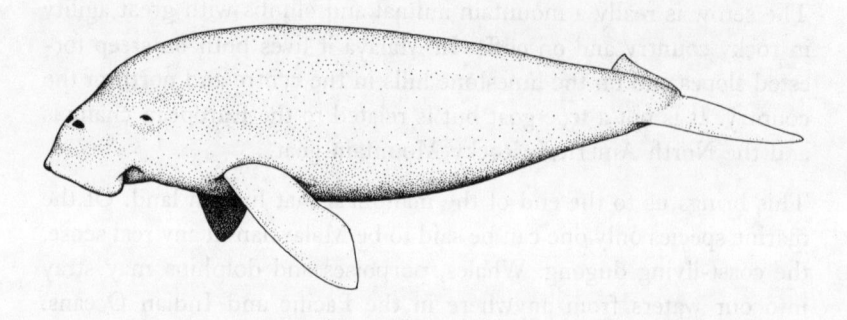

Fig. 15. Dugong.

DUGONG *(Dugong dugon)* Fig. 15
DUYUNG

Length up to 3 metres, males larger than females and also distinguished by possessing a pair of tusks in the upper jaw. The skin is greyish brown and almost hairless except for some bristles on the snout. The paddles are fairly small and the tail is divided into two flukes just like that of a whale or porpoise.

Dugongs live in shallow water and feed on seaweeds and marine grass *(Enhalus)* growing on the bottom. They have an acute sense of hearing and may communicate by underwater sound pulses as whales do. They have never been common in Malaysian waters and are now certainly rare and may be extinct or on the verge of extinction. They may still survive in fair numbers around the coasts of New Guinea and tropical Australia, but are in need of protection wherever they occur.

CETACEA
WHALES, DOLPHINS, PORPOISES

Although they cannot be regarded as Malaysian a great variety of these purely marine mammals may be seen by travellers in our surrounding seas and are occasionally stranded on our coasts. One notable stranding occurred in 1954 on the coast of Malacca, a specimen of Stejneger's Beaked Whale *(Mesoplodon stejnegeri)*, a great rarity of which only five specimens had been previously recorded, one of them from Siberia and two from New Zealand! This seems to imply that almost any species of whale may swim into Malaysian seas at one time or another.

In his book on the mammals of Singapore and Malaya Professor Harrison gave a list of 'likely species', the cetaceans that the voyager in Malaysian seas is most likely to see. I reproduce this below with two additions. The plumbeous dolphin is said to be fairly common off the northern Bornean coast, and five specimens of Bryde's whale have been reported from the region. In Malay whales are IKAN PAUS, dolphins and porpoises LOMBA LOMBA.

BRYDE'S WHALE *(Balaenoptera edeni)*

Length 12–14 metres. This is one of the smaller of the whalebone whales, so called because they lack teeth, in place of which plates of horny baleen or whalebone are grown in the jaws. These plates fray into bristles at the edge and are used to strain out the small animals on which the whales feed. The food of the largest whales, including the enormous blue whale, is mainly shrimps, but Bryde's whale feeds on fish up to 30 cm long, and its baleen plates are short with coarse bristles. It can be recognised, if stranded, by the elongate head, baleen plates and conspicuous longitudinal grooves on the under side of the head and fore part of the body. These features are also seen in other species of *Balaenoptera* or rorquals, and Bryde's whale is distinguished from these by the presence of three ridges along the top of the head.

Five stranded whales of this species have been identified on Malaysian coasts, the last on the Selangor coast in 1972, and some older records of uncertain identity may well be of Bryde's whales. Unlike the other baleen whales it seems to be confined to tropical seas.

SPERM WHALE *(Physeter catodon)*

Males reach 20 metres, females seldom as much as half this length. The huge blunt-nosed head, narrow lower jaw and large teeth distinguish this from all the other big whales. At sea little is seen of it but the 'spout' or 'blow' (really a spray of exhalent breath) which is distinctive in being directed obliquely forwards, not vertical. This whale feeds by diving deeply and hunting large squids. It was formerly abundant in the warmer seas, but the brutal compulsive greed of the whaling industry has reduced its numbers sadly, as it has of that of all the great whales.

INDIAN PILOT WHALE *(Globicephala macrorhyncha)* Fig. 16

With a length up to five metres this animal can be regarded as a small whale or a large porpoise. It is entirely black with a rather low dorsal fin in front of the middle of the body and a curiously swollen forehead which bulges out above the upper jaw. It swims in shoals or 'schools' and sometimes whole schools of a dozen whales or more strand themselves and die in what looks like mass suicide.

IRRAWADDY DOLPHIN *(Orcaella brevirostris)* Fig. 17

Length a little over two metres, grey with a small dorsal fin well behind the middle of the body. The head is globular, rather like that of the Indian pilot whale, from which its small size and the position of the dorsal fin distinguish it.

The English name is ill-chosen. The term 'dolphin' is a convenient one to define the small cetaceans with beaked jaws, and although this one does enter the Irrawaddy River in Burma it is widespread around the coasts of south-eastern Asia.

FINLESS BLACK PORPOISE *(Neomeris phocanoides)* Fig. 18

A small cetacean, $1\frac{1}{2}$ metres long, black, with a round blunt head and lacking any dorsal fin. It frequents river estuaries as well as the open sea.

COMMON DOLPHIN *(Delphinus delphis)* Fig. 19

Length $2\frac{1}{2}$ metres. Brown or grey above, pale grey below, sometimes with a distinct pattern of stripes along the flanks. There is a fairly

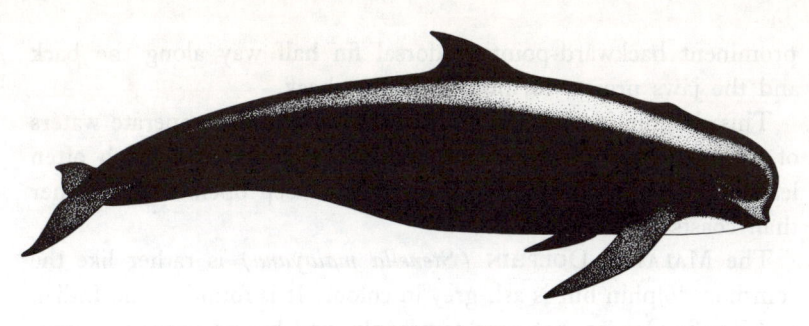

Fig. 16. Indian Pilot Whale.

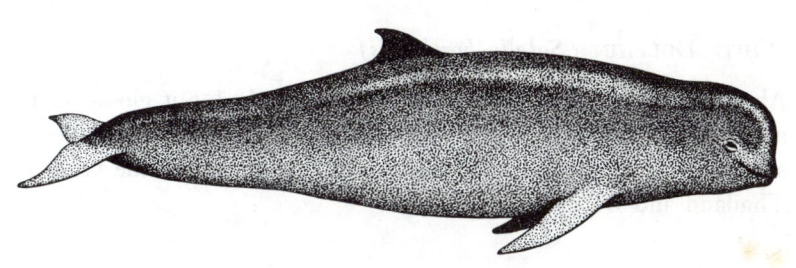

Fig. 17. Irrawaddy Dolphin.

Fig. 18. Finless Black Porpoise.

Fig. 19. Common Dolphin.

prominent backward-pointing dorsal fin half way along the back and the jaws project forming a distinct beak.

This dolphin is common all over the warm and temperate waters of the world and swims in shoals of several hundreds which often leap and play around ships. It frequents deep open waters rather than coasts and estuaries.

The MALAYAN DOLPHIN *(Stenella malayana)* is rather like the common dolphin but is ash-grey in colour. It is found in the Indian and Pacific Oceans, not very commonly, and has no particular association with Malaya.

WHITE DOLPHIN *(Sotalia borneensis)*

About as big as a common dolphin and also beaked, but glossy white above dappled with grey, and with a fairly low dorsal fin. It frequents shallow seas and seems to be seen most often between the Gulf of Thailand and Borneo.

PLUMBEOUS DOLPHIN *(Sousa plumbea)*

Length $2\frac{1}{2}$ metres. 'Plumbeous' means lead-coloured, and it is a uniform lead grey with a white patch under the chin. The beak is long, about a sixth of the total length. In Malaysian waters it is seen most often off the coast of Borneo.

A CHECK LIST OF MALAYSIAN MAMMALS

The following list has been complied from the two books by Lord Medway: *The Wild Mammals of Malaya,* Oxford University Press, 1969, and *Mammals of Borneo,* Malaysian Branch Royal Asiatic Society, Second Edition, 1977. Since both West and East Malaysia are covered by the one list I have indicated by the insertions 'MALAYA' or 'BORNEO' those species that occur in the one territory but not in the other; where there is no such indication the species is common to the two territories. The indication 'END.' (endemic) is added for those species that have been recorded only from the Malay Peninsula or only from Borneo and appear to be confined to one or the other. It will be noted that there are far more endemic species in Borneo and the great majority of these are probably true endemics; in the case of Malaya most of the species indicated as such are more likely to be rarities which await discovery elsewhere in south-eastern Asia. The Cetacea (dolphins and whales) have no territorial association with Malaysia and are not included in the check list.

All the specific names are accompanied by the name of the author who originally described and named the species. The author's name is put in brackets if he did not use the same generic name as that now considered appropriate. Thus: *Elephas maximus* Linnaeus, but *Panthera pardus* (Linnaeus) because Linnaeus originally gave the leopard the name *Felis pardus*.

ORDER INSECTIVORA

FAMILY ERINACEIDAE

Echinosorex gymnurus (Raffles)   Moonrat or Gymnure
Hylomys suillus Müller   Lesser Gymnure

FAMILY TALPIDAE

Talpa micrura Hodgson   Short-tailed Mole   MALAYA

FAMILY SORICIDAE

Suncus murinus (Linnaeus)   House Shrew
Suncus ater Medway   Black Shrew   BORNEO END.
Suncus etruscus (Savi)   Savi's Pigmy Shrew
Crocidura fuliginosa (Blyth)   South-east Asian White-toothed Shrew
Chimarrogale himalayica (Gray)   Himalayan Water Shrew

FAMILY TUPAIIDAE

Ptilocercus lowii Gray   Pentail Treeshrew
Tupaia glis (Diard)   Common Treeshrew
Tupaia minor Gunther   Lesser Treeshrew
Tupaia splendidula Gray   Ruddy Treeshrew   BORNEO END.
Tupaia montana Thomas   Mountain Treeshrew   BORNEO END.
Tupaia gracilis Thomas   Slender Treeshrew   BORNEO END.
Tupaia picta Thomas   Painted Treeshrew   BORNEO END.
Tupaia dorsalis Schlegel   Striped Treeshrew   BORNEO END.
Tupaia tana Raffles   Large Treeshrew   BORNEO
Dendrogale melanura Thomas   Smooth-tailed Treeshrew   BORNEO END.

ORDER DERMOPTERA

FAMILY CYNOCEPHALIDAE

Cynocephalus variegatus (Audebert)   Colugo or Flying Lemur

ORDER CHIROPTERA

FAMILY PTEROPIDAE

Rousettus amplexicaudatus (Geoffroy)   Geoffroy's Rousette Bat
Pteropus vampyrus (Linnaeus)   Large Flying Fox
Pteropus hypomelanus Temminck   Island Flying Fox
Cynopterus brachyotis (Müller)   Malaysian Fruit Bat
Cynopterus horsfieldi Gray   Horsfield's Fruit Bat
Megaerops ecaudatus (Temminck)   Tailless Fruit Bat
Dyacopterus spadiceus (Thomas)   Dyak Fruit Bat
Balionycteris maculata (Thomas)   Spotted-winged Fruit Bat
Chironax melanocephalus (Temminck)   Black-capped Fruit Bat
   MALAYA
Aethalops alecto (Thomas)   Grey Fruit Bat
Pentethor lucasii (Dobson)   Dusky Fruit Bat
Eonycteris spelea (Dobson)   Cave Fruit Bat
Eonycteris major Anderson   Dulit Fruit Bat   BORNEO END.
Macroglossus lagochilus Matschie   Common Long-tongued Fruit Bat
Macroglossus minimus (Geoffroy)   Hill Long-tongued Fruit Bat
   MALAYA

FAMILY EMBALLONURIDAE

Emballonura monticola Temminck   Lesser Sheath-tailed Bat
Emballonura alecto (Eydoux & Gervais) Greater Sheath-tailed Bat
   BORNEO
Taphozous melanopogon Temminck   Black-bearded Tomb Bat
Taphozous longimanus Hardwicke   Long-winged or Pied Tomb Bat
Taphozous saccolaimus Temminck   Pouch-bearing Bat

FAMILY MEGADERMATIDAE

Megaderma spasma (Linnaeus)   Malayan False Vampire
Megaderma lyra Geoffroy   Indian False Vampire   MALAYA

FAMILY NYCTERIDIDAE

Nycteris javanica Geoffroy   Hollow-faced Bat

FAMILY RHINOLOPHIDAE

Rhinolophus affinis Horsfield   Intermediate Horseshoe Bat
Rhinolophus sedulus Andersen   Lesser Woolly Horseshoe Bat
Rhinolophus trifoliatus Temminck   Trefoil Horseshoe Bat
Rhinolophus luctus Temminck   Great Eastern Horseshoe Bat
Rhinolophus stheno Andersen   Lesser Brown Horseshoe Bat   MALAYA
Rhinolophus robinsoni Andersen   Peninsular Horseshoe Bat   MALAYA
Rhinolophus refulgens Andersen   Glossy Horseshoe Bat   MALAYA
Rhinolophus minutillus Miller   Least Horseshoe Bat   MALAYA
Rhinolophus macrotis Blyth   Big-eared Horseshoe Bat   MALAYA
Rhinolophus coelophyllus Peters   Croslet Horseshoe Bat   MALAYA
Rhinolophus malayanus Bonhote   Northern Malayan Horseshoe Bat   MALAYA
Rhinolophus borneensis Peters   Borneo Horseshoe Bat   BORNEO
Rhinolophus arcuatus Peters   Arcuate Horseshoe Bat   BORNEO
Rhinolophus acuminatus Peters   Acuminate Horseshoe Bat   BORNEO
Rhinolophus philippinensis Waterhouse   Philippine Horseshoe Bat   BORNEO
Hipposideros bicolor Temminck   Bicolour Roundleaf Horseshoe Bat   MALAYA
Hipposideros sabanus Thomas   Lawas Roundleaf Horseshoe Bat
Hipposideros cineraceus Blyth   Least Roundleaf Horseshoe Bat
Hipposideros galeritus Cantor   Common or Cantor's Roundleaf Horseshoe Bat

Hipposideros larvatus (Horsfield)   Large Roundleaf Horseshoe Bat
Hipposideros diadema Geoffroy   Diadem Roundleaf Horseshoe Bat
Hipposideros lylei (Thomas)   Shield-faced Bat   MALAYA
Hipposideros armiger (Hodgson)   Great Roundleaf Horseshoe Bat   MALAYA
Hipposideros ridleyi Robinson & Kloss   Singapore Roundleaf Horseshoe Bat   MALAYA END.
Hipposideros nequam Andersen   Malayan Roundleaf Horseshoe Bat   MALAYA END.
Hipposideros dyacorum Thomas   Dayak Roundleaf Horseshoe Bat   BORNEO END.
Hipposideros coxi Shelford   Cox's Roundleaf Horseshoe Bat   BORNEO END.
Aselliscus stoliczkanus (Dobson)   Trident Horseshoe Bat   MALAYA
Coelops robinsoni Bonhote   Malayan Tailless Horseshoe Bat   MALAYA
Coelops frithii Blyth   East Asian Tailless Horseshoe Bat   MALAYA

FAMILY VESPERTILIONIDAE

Myotis mystacinus (Kuhl)   Whiskered Bat
Myotis hasseltii (Temminck)   Lesser Large-footed or Van Hasselt's Bat
Myotis adversus Horsfield   Large-footed or Grey Long-footed Bat
Myotis horsfieldi (Temminck)   Horsfield's Bat
Myotis macrotarsus Waterhouse   Long-footed Bat   BORNEO
Myotis siligorensis (Tomes)   Himalayan Whiskered Bat   MALAYA
Myotis montivagus (Dobson)   Burmese Whiskered Bat   MALAYA
Myotis oreias (Temminck)   Singapore Whiskered Bat   MALAYA END.

Nyctalus noctula (Schreber)   Noctule   MALAYA (doubtful record)
Pipistrellus stenopterus (Dobson)   Malaysian Noctule
Pipistrellus imbricatus (Horsfield)   Brown Pipistrelle   MALAYA
Pipistrellus ridleyi Thomas   Malay Pipistrelle   MALAYA END.
Pipistrellus ceylonicus (Kelaart)   Kelaart's Pipistrelle   BORNEO
Pipistrellus kitcheneri Thomas   Dark Brown Pipistrelle   BORNEO END.
Pipistrellus javanicus (Gray)   Javan Pipistrelle
Pipistrellus tenuis (Temminck)   Least or Slender Pipistrelle
Glischropus tylopus (Dobson)   Thick-thumbed Pipistrelle
Philetor branchypterus (Temminck)   Short-winged Brown Bat
Hesperoptenus blanfordi (Dobson)   Blanford's Bat or Lesser False Serotine   MALAYA
Hesperoptenus tomesi (Thomas)   Large False Serotine
Hesperopternus doriae   False Serotine   BORNEO
Tylonycteris robustula Thomas   Greater Flat-headed Bat
Tylonycteris pachypus (Temminck)   Lesser Flat-headed Bat
Scotophilus kuhlii Leach   House Bat
Murina suilla (Temminck)   Brown or Lesser Tube-nosed Bat
Murina aenea Hill   Bronzed Tube-nosed Bat   MALAYA END.
Murina huttoni (Peters)   Hutton's Tube-nosed Bat   MALAYA
Murina cyclotis Dobson   Round-eared Tube-nosed Bat   MALAYA
Harpiocephalus harpia (Temminck)   Hairy-winged Bat   BORNEO
Kerivoula hardwickii (Horsfield)   Hardwicke's Bat
Kerivoula pellucida (Waterhouse)   Clear-winged Bat
Kerivoula minuta Miller   Least Forest Bat
Kerivoula papillosa (Temminck)   Papillose Bat
Kerivoula picta (Pallas)   Painted Bat   MALAYA
Kerivoula whiteheadi Thomas   Little Forest Bat   BORNEO
Phoniscus jagorii (Thomas)   Large Groove-toothed Bat   BORNEO
Phoniscus atrox (Miller)   Small Groove-toothed Bat   MALAYA
Miniopterus schreibersii (Kuhl)   Schreibers' Bat

Miniopterus medius Thomas & Wroughton   South-east Asian or Medium Bent-winged Bat
Miniopterus australis Tomes   Lesser Bent-winged Bat   BORNEO

FAMILY MOLOSSIDAE

Tadarida mops (de Blainville)   Free-tailed Bat
Tadarida plicata (Buchannan)   Wrinkle-lipped Bat
Tadarida johorensis (Dobson)   Dato Meldrum's Bat
Cheiromeles torquatus Horsfield   Hairless Bat

ORDER PRIMATES

FAMILY LORISIDAE

Nycticebus coucang (Boddaert)   Slow Loris

FAMILY TARSIIDAE

Tarsius bancanus Horsfield   Western Tarsier   BORNEO

FAMILY CERCOPITHECIDAE

Presbytis cristata (Raffles)   Silvered Leaf Monkey
Presbytis melalophus (Raffles)   Banded Leaf Monkey
Presbytis obscura (Reid)   Dusky or Spectacled Leaf Monkey   MALAYA
Presbytis hosei (Thomas)   Grey Leaf Monkey   BORNEO END.
Presbytis rubicunda (Müller)   Maroon Leaf Monkey   BORNEO END.
Presbytis frontata (Müller)   White-fronted Leaf Monkey   BORNEO END.
Nasalis larvatus (van Wurmb)   Proboscis Monkey   BORNEO END.
Macaca fascicularis (Raffles)   Long-tailed Macaque
Macaca nemestrina (Linnacus)   Pig-tailed Macaque
Macaca speciosa Cuvier   Stump-tailed Macaque   MALAYA

FAMILY PONGIDAE

Hylobates agilis Cuvier   Agile Gibbon
Hylobates lar (Linnaeus)   White-handed or Lar Gibbon
  MALAYA
Hylobates syndactylus (Raffles)   Siamang   MALAYA
Hylobates muelleri Martin   Borneo Gibbon   BORNEO END.
Pongo pygmaeus (Linnaeus)   Orang-utan   BORNEO

ORDER PHOLIDOTA

FAMILY MANIDAE

Manis javanica Desmarest   Pangolin or Scaly Ant-eater

ORDER RODENTIA

FAMILY SCIURIDAE

Ratufa affinis (Raffles)   Cream-coloured Giant Squirrel
Ratufa bicolor (Sparrman)   Black Giant Squirrel   MALAYA
Callosciurus prevostii (Desmarest)   Prevost's Squirrel
Callosciurus baluensis (Bonhote)   Kinabalu Squirrel
  BORNEO END.
Callosciurus notatus (Boddaert)   Plantain Squirrel
Callosciurus nigrovittatus (Horsfield)   Black-banded Squirrel
Callosciurus caniceps (Gray)   Grey-bellied Squirrel
  MALAYA
Callosciurus flavimanus (Geoffroy)   Mountain Red-bellied
  Squirrel   MALAYA
Callosciurus adamsi (Kloss)   Ear-spot Squirrel   BORNEO
  END.
Sundasciurus hippurus (Geoffroy)   Horse-tailed Squirrel
Sundasciurus tenuis (Horsfield)   Slender Squirrel
Sundasciurus lowii (Thomas)   Low's Squirrel
Sundasciurus jentinki (Thomas)   Jentink's Squirrel
  BORNEO END.

Sundasciurus brookei (Thomas)   Brooke's Squirrel
BORNEO END.
Glyphotes simus Thomas   Red-bellied Sculptor Squirrel
BORNEO END.
Glyphotes canalvus Moore   Grey-bellied Sculptor Squirrel
BORNEO END.
Tamiops macclellandii (Horsfield)   Himalayan Striped Squirrel
MALAYA
Lariscus insignis (Cuvier)   Three-striped Ground Squirrel
Lariscus hosei (Thomas)   Four-striped Ground Squirrel
BORNEO END.
Dremomys rufigenis (Blanford)   Red-cheeked Ground Squirrel
MALAYA
Dremomys everetti (Thomas)   Bornean Mountain Ground Squirrel   BORNEO END.
Rhinosciurus laticaudatus (Müller)   Shrew-faced Ground Squirrel
Nannosciurus melanotis (Müller)   Black-eared Pigmy Squirrel
BORNEO
Exilisciurus exilis (Müller)   Plain Pigmy Squirrel   BORNEO END.
Exilisciurus whiteheadi (Thomas)   Whitehead's Pigmy Squirrel
BORNEO END.
Rheithosciurus macrotis (Gray)   Tufted Ground Squirrel
BORNEO END.
Petaurillus kinlochii (Robinson & Kloss)   Selangor Pigmy Flying Squirrel   MALAYA END.
Petaurillus hosei (Thomas)   Hose's Pigmy Flying Squirrel
BORNEO END.
Petaurillus emiliae (Thomas)   Lesser Pigmy Flying Squirrel
BORNEO END.
Iomys horsfieldi (Waterhouse)   Horsfield's Flying Squirrel
Aeromys tephromelas (Günther)   Black Flying Squirrel
Aeromys thomasi (Hose)   Thomas's Flying Squirrel   BORNEO END.
Petinomys setosus (Temminck)   Temminck's Flying Squirrel
Petinomys vordermanni (Jentink)   Vordermann's Flying Squirrel
Petinomys genibarbis (Horsfield)   Whiskered Flying Squirrel

Petinomys hageni (Jentink)   Hagen's Flying Squirrel
  BORNEO
Hylopetes lepidus (Horsfield)   Grey-cheeked Flying Squirrel
Hylopetes spadiceus (Blyth)   Red-cheeked Flying Squirrel
Pteromyscus pulverulentus (Günther)   Smoky Flying Squirrel
Petaurista petaurista (Pallas)   Red Giant Flying Squirrel
Petaurista elegans (Müller)   Spotted Giant Flying Squirrel

FAMILY RHIZOMIDAE

Rhizomys sumatrensis (Raffles)   Large Bamboo Rat   MALAYA
Rhizomys pruinosus Blyth   Hoary Bamboo Rat   MALAYA

FAMILY MURIDAE

Rattus rattus (Linnaeus)   House Rat
Rattus tiomanicus (Miller)   Malaysian Field Rat or Wood Rat
Rattus argentiventer (Robinson & Kloss)   Ricefield Rat
Rattus exulans (Peale)   Polynesian Rat
Rattus norvegicus (Berkenhout)   Norway Rat
Rattus baluensis (Thomas)   Summit Rat   BORNEO END.
Rattus annandalei (Bonhote)   Annandale's Rat   MALAYA
Rattus muelleri (Jentink)   Müller's rat
Rattus cremoriventer (Miller)   Dark-tailed Tree Rat
Rattus bowersii (Anderson)   Bowers' Rat   MALAYA
Rattus infraluteus (Thomas)   Mountain Giant Rat   BORNEO
Rattus rapit (Bonhote)   Long-tailed Mountain Rat   BORNEO
Rattus fulvescens (Gray)   Chestnut Rat   MALAYA
Rattus niviventer (Hodgson)   White-bellied Rat   MALAYA
Rattus rajah (Thomas)   Brown Spiny Rat
Rattus surifer (Miller)   Red Spiny Rat
Rattus inas (Bonhote)   Malayan Mountain Spiny Rat
  MALAYA END.
Rattus alticola (Thomas)   Mountain Spiny Rat   BORNEO
  END.
Rattus ochraceiventer (Thomas)   Chestnut-bellied Spiny Rat
  BORNEO END.

Rattus baedon (Thomas)   Small Spiny Rat   BORNEO END.
Rattus whiteheadi (Thomas)   Whitehead's Rat
Rattus sabanus (Thomas)   Long-tailed Giant Rat
Lenothrix canus Miller   Grey Tree Rat
Mus musculus Linnaeus   House Mouse
Mus caroli Bonhote   MALAYA
Chiropodomys gliroidies (Blyth)   Common Pencil-tailed Tree Mouse
Chiropodomys major Thomas   Large Pencil-tailed Tree Mouse   BORNEO END.
Chiropodomys muroides Medway   Grey-bellied Pencil-tailed Tree Mouse   BORNEO END.
Hapalomys longicaudatus Blyth   Marmoset Rat   MALAYA
Pithecheir melanurus Cuvier   Monkey-footed Rat   MALAYA
Haeromys margarettae (Thomas)   Ranee Mouse   BORNEO END.
Haeromys pusillus (Thomas)   Lesser Ranee Mouse   BORNEO END.

FAMILY HYSTRICIDAE

Hystrix brachyura Linnaeus   Common or Malayan Porcupine
Thecurus crassispinis (Günther)   Thick-spined Porcupine   BORNEO
Trichys lipura Günther   Long-tailed Porcupine
Atherurus macrourus (Linnaeus)   Brush-tailed Porcupine   MALAYA

ORDER CARNIVORA
FAMILY CANIDAE

Cuon alpinus (Pallas)   Red Dog or Dhole   MALAYA

FAMILY URSIDAE

Helarctos malayanus (Raffles)   Sun Bear

FAMILY MUSTELIDAE

Martes flavigula (Boddaert)   Yellow-throated Marten
Musttla nudipes Desmarest   Malay Weasel
Melogale orientalis (Horsfield)   Ferret Badger   BORNEO
Mydaus javanensis (Leschenault)   Teledu or Malay Badger   BORNEO
Lutra sumatrana (Gray)   Hairy-nosed Otter
Lutra perspicillata Geoffroy   Smooth Otter
Lutra lutra (Linnaeus) Common Otter   MALAYA
Amblonyx cinerea (Illiger)   Oriental Small-clawed Otter

FAMILY VIVERRIDAE

Viverra tangalunga Gray   Malay Civet
Viverra zibetha Linnaeus   Large Indian Civet   MALAYA
Viverra megaspila Blyth   Large Spotted Civet   MALAYA
Viverra malaccensis (Gmelin)   Little Civet   MALAYA
Prionodon linsang (Hardwicke)   Banded Linsang
Paradoxurus hermaphroditus (Pallas)   Common Palm Civet
Paguma larvata (Hamilton-Smith)   Masked Palm Civet
Arctitis binturung (Raffles)   Binturung or Bearcat
Arctogalidia trivirgata (Gray)   Small-toothed Palm Civet
Hemigalus derbyanus (Gray)   Banded Palm Civet
Hemigalus hosei (Thomas)   Hose's Civet   BORNEO END.
Cynogale bennetti Gray   Otter-Civet
Herpestes brachyurus Gray   Short-tailed Mongoose
Herpestes semitorquatus Gray   Collared Mongoose   BORNEO
Herpestes hosei Jentink   Hose's Mongoose   BORNEO END.
Herpestes edwardsii (Geoffory)   Indian Grey Mongoose   MALAYA
Herpestes auropunctatus (Hodgson)   Small Indian Mongoose   MALAYA
Herpestes javanicus (Geoffroy)   Javan Mongoose   MALAYA

FAMILY FELIDAE

Panthera tigris (Linnaeus)   Tiger   MALAYA
Panthera pardus (Linnaeus)   Leopard or Panther   MALAYA

Neofelis nebulosa (Griffith)   Clouded Leopard
Felis benegalensis Kerr   Leopard Cat
Felis marmorata Martin   Marbled Cat
Felis planiceps Vigors & Horsfield   Flat-headed Cat
Felis temminckii Vigors & Horsfield   Golden Cat   MALAYA
Felis badia Gray   Bay Cat   BORNEO END.

ORDER SIRENIA
FAMILY DUGONGIDAE
Dugong dugon (Miller)   Dugong

ORDER PROBOSCIDEA
FAMILY ELEPHANTIDAE
Elephas maximus Linnaeus   Indian Elephant   MALAYA
(doubtfully indigenous in Borneo)

ORDER PERISSODACTYLA
FAMILY TAPIRIDAE
Tapirus indicus Desmarest   Malay Tapir   MALAYA
(probably extinct in Borneo)

FAMILY RHINOCEROTIDAE
Didermocerus sumatrensis (Fischer)   Sumatran or Asiatic Two-horned Rhinoceros
Rhinoceros sondaicus Desmarest   Javan or Lesser One-horned Rhinoceros   MALAYA   (recently extinct)

ORDER ARTIODACTYLA
FAMILY SUIDAE

Sus scrofa Linnaeus   Wild Pig   MALAYA
Sus barbatus Müller   Bearded Pig

FAMILY TRAGULIDAE

Tragulus javanicus (Osbeck)   Lesser Mouse Deer
Tragulus napu (Cuvier)   Large Mouse Deer

FAMILY CERVIDAE

Muntiacus muntjak (Zimmermann)   Barking Deer
Cervus unicolor Kerr   Sambar
Cervus timorensis Blainville   Javan Rusa   BORNEO

FAMILY BOVIDAE

Bos gaurus Smith   Gaur   MALAYA
Bos javanicus d'Alton   Banteng or Temadau
Capricornis sumatraensis (Bechstein)   Serow   MALAYA

INDEX

ENGLISH NAMES *are in ordinary type*
MALAY NAMES **are in bold type**
LATIN NAMES *are in italic type*
FAMILIES *are in small capitals*

Aeromys tephromelas, 35
Aeromys thomasi, 35
Aetherurus macrourus, 41
Amblonyx cinerea, 54
APES, 26
Arctitis binturong, 50
Arctogalidia trivirgata, 50
ARTIODACTYLA, 55, 59

Babi bodoh, 59
Babi hutan, 59
Babi jokut, 59
Badak berendam, 57
Badak murai, 58
Badger, Malayan stink, 55
BADGERS, 53
Balaenoptera edeni, 65
Bambun ekor pendek, 52
Banteng, 62
Bat, black-bearded tomb, 17
Bat, cave fruit, 14
Bat, common long-tongued, 14
Bat, common roundleaf horseshoe, 15
Bat, diadem roundleaf horseshoe, 15
Bat, hairless, 19
Bat, Horsfield's fruit, 14
Bat, house, 18
Bat, lesser flat-headed, 18
Bat, Malaysian fruit, 14
Bat, whiskered, 18
Bat, wrinkle-lipped 19
Batin kelasar, 19
BATS, 11
Bear, Malayan sun, 44
Bearcat, 50
Berang-berang, 54
Beruang, 44
Beruk, 23
Binturong, 50
Binturung, 50

Bos gaurus, 62
Bos javanicus, 62
BOVIDAE, 61

Callosciurus adamsi, 31
Callosciurus caniceps, 30
Callosciurus flavimanus, 30
Callosciurus nigrovittatus, 31
Callosciurus notatus, 30
Callosciurus prevostii, 31
Canis, 43
Capricornis sumatraensis, 62
CARNIVORA, 43
Cat, bay, 47
Cat, flat-headed, 47
Cat, golden, 47
Cat, leopard, 47
Cat, marbled, 47
Cat, toddy, 49
CATS, 44
Cecadu besar, 14
Cecadu gua, 14
Cecadu pisang, 14
Cencurut hutan, 8
Cencurut rumah, 8
Ceneka, 24
Cenkung, 24
CERVIDAE, 60
Cervus unicolor, 61
CETACEA, 64
Cheiromeles torquatus, 19
CHEVROTAINS, 60
Chiropodomys glirioides, 39
CHIROPTERA, 11
Cipan, 58
Civet, banded palm, 52
Civet, common palm, 49
Civet, large Indian, 48
Civet, large spotted, 49
Civet, little, 49
Civet, Malay, 48, 49

Civet, masked, palm, 50
Civet, otter, 52
Civet, small-toothed, 50
Civet, three-striped palm, 50
CIVETS, 47
Colugo, Malayan, 20
COLUGOS, 19
Crocidura fuliginosa, 8
Cuon alpinus, 43
Cynocephalus variegatus, 20
Cynogale bennettii, 52
Cynopterus brachyotis, 14
Cynopterus horsfieldi, 14

DEER, 60
Deer, barking, 61
Dekan, 39
Delphinus delphis, 66
DERMOPTERA, 19
Dhole, 43
Didermocerus sumatrensis, 57
Dog, red, 43
Dolphin, common, 66, 67
Dolphin, Irrawaddy, 66, 67
Dolphin, Malayan, 68
Dolphin, plumbeous, 68
Dolphin, white, 68
DOLPHINS, 64
Dugong, 63, 64
Dugong dugon, 64
Duyung, 64

Echinosorex gymnurus, 6
Elephant, Indian, 56
Elephas maximus, 56
Eonycteris spelaea, 14
Exilisciurus exilis, 32
Exilisciurus whiteheadi, 32

Felis badia, 47
Felis bengalensis, 47
Felis marmorata, 47
Felis planiceps, 47
Felis temminckii, 47
Ferret-badger, Javanese, 54
Flying fox, island, 13
Flying fox, large, 13
FLYING LEMURS, 19
FLYING SQUIRRELS, 34

FRUIT BATS, 13

Gajah, 56
Gaur, 62
Gibbon, agile, 27
Gibbon Bornean, 27
Gibbon, dark-handed, 27
Gibbon white-handed, 27
Globicephala macrorhyncha, 66
Gymnure, 6
Gymnure, lesser, 7

Haeromys, 39
Harimau belang, 45
Harimau bintang, 46
Harimau dahan, 46
Harimau kumbang, 46
Helarctos malayanus, 44
Hemigalus derbyanus, 52
HERBIVORES, 55
Herpestes brachyurus, 52
Herpestes hosei, 53
Herpestes javanicus, 53
Hipposideros diadema, 16
Hipposideros galeritus, 15
Hylobates agilis, 27
Hylobates lar, 26
Hylobates muelleri, 27
Hylobates syndactylus, 27
Hylomys suillus, 7
Hylopetes spadiceus, 35
Hystrix brachyura, 41

INSECTIVORA, 6
Iomys horsfieldii, 35

Kambing gurun, 62
Kancil, 60
Kelawar buluh kecil, 18
Kelawar dagu hitam, 17
Kelawar daun pisang, 18
Kelawar ladam bulat gua, 15
Kelawar rumah, 18
Kelawar telinga lebar, 17
Keluang, 13
Kera, 23
Kera belanda, 25
Kera hantu, 22
Kerawak hitam, 32

84

Kerawak putih-kuning, 32
Kijang, 61
Kongkang, 21
Kubung, 20
Kucing batu, 47

Landak batu, 42
Landak Borneo, 41
Landak kelubi, 42
Landak nibong, 42
Landak padi, 42
Landak raya, 41
Landak tunggal, 41
Lariscus insignis, 33
Leopard, 46
Leopard, clouded, 46
Linsang, banded, 50, 51
Lomba-lomba, 65
Loris, slow, 21
Lotong, 24
Lotong bangkatan, 25
Lutra lutra, 54
Lutra perspicillata, 54
Lutra sumatrana, 54

Macaca fascicularis, 23
Macaca nemestrina, 23
Macaca speciosa, 24
Macaque, long-tailed, 23
Macaque, pig-tailed, 23
Macaque, stump-tailed, 24
Macroglossus lagochilus, 14
Manatee, 63
Manis javanica, 28
Marten, yellow-throated, 53
Martes flavigula, 53
Mawas, 27
MEGACHIROPTERA, 13
Megaderma lyra, 17
Megaderma spasma, 17
Melogale orientalis, 54
Mengkira, 53
Mesoplodon stejnegeri, 65
MICE, 35
Mice, ranee, 39
MICROCHIROPTERA, 15
Mole, short-tailed, 7
Mongoose, Hose's, 53
Mongoose, Javan, 53

Mongoose, short-tailed, 52
MONGOOSES, 47
Monkey, banded leaf, 24
Monkey, maroon leaf, 24
Monkey, proboscis, 25
Monkey, silvered leaf, 24
MONKEYS, 22
Moonrat, 6
Mouse, house, 37
MOUSE-DEER, 60
Mouse-deer, large, 60
Mouse-deer, lesser, 60
Muntiacus muntjak, 61
Muntjac, Indian, 61
Mus musculus, 37
Musang akar, 50
Musang pulut, 49
Mustela nudipes, 54
MUSTELIDAE, 53
Mydaus javanicus, 55
Myotis mystacinus, 18

Napoh, 60
Nasalis larvatus, 25
Neofelis nebulosa, 46
Neomeris phocanoides, 66
Noctule, Malaysian, 18
Nyctalus stenopterus, 18
Nycticebus coucang, 21

Orang-utan, 27
Orcaella brevirostris, 66
Otter, common, 54
Otter, hairy-nosed, 54
Otter, small-clawed, 54
Otter, smooth, 54
OTTERS, 53

Paguma larvata, 50
Pangolin Malayan, 28
Panther, 46
Panthera pardus, 46
Panthera tigris, 45
Paradoxurus hermaphroditus, 49
Paus, ikan, 65
Pelanduk, 60
PERISSODACTYLA, 55, 57
Petaurista elegans, 35
Petaurista petaurista, 34

Pig, bearded, 59
Pig, wild, 59
Pipistrellus stenopterus, 18
PHOLIDOTA, 28
Physeter catodon, 65
Pongo pygmaeus, 27
Porcupine, brush-tailed, 41
Porcupine, long-tailed, 42
Porcupine, Malayan, 41
Porcupine, thick-spined, 41
PORCUPINES, 40
Porpoise, finless black, 66, 67
PORPOISES, 64
Presbytis cristata, 24
Presbytis melalophos, 24
Presbytis obscura, 24
Presbytis rubicunda, 24
PRIMATES, 20
Prionodon linsang, 50
PROBOSCIDEA, 55, 56
Pteropus hypomelanus, 13
Pteropus vampyrus, 13
Ptilocercus lowii, 10
Pulasan, 54
Pulasan lamri, 54

Rat, Bowers', 38
Rat, brown spiny, 39
Rat, hoary bamboo, 40
Rat, house, 36
Rat, large bamboo, 39
Rat, little, 37
Rat, long-tailed giant, 38
Rat, Malaysian field, 37
Rat, Mueller's, 38
Rat, Norway, 36
Rat, Polynesian, 37
Rat, rajah, 39
Rat, red spiny, 39
Rat, ricefield, 37
Rat, wood, 37
RATS, 35
Rattus argentiventer, 37
Rattus bowersi, 38
Rattus exulans, 37
Rattus muelleri, 38
Rattus norvegicus, 36
Rattus rajah, 39
Rattus rattus, 36, 37

Rattus sabanus, 38
Rattus surifer, 39
Rattus tiomanicus, 37
Ratufa affinis, 32
Ratufa bicolor, 32
Rhinoceros, Javan, 58
Rhinoceros sondaicus, 58
Rhinoceros, Sumatran, 57
Rhinosciurus laticaudatus, 34
Rhizomys sumatrensis, 39
Rhizomys pruinosus, 40
RODENTIA, 29
Rousette, Geoffroy's, 14
Rousettus amplexicaudatus, 14
Rusa, 61

Sambar, 61
Scotophilus kuhlii, 18
Sea cow, Steller's, 63
Seladang, 62
Serigala, 43
Serow, 62
Shrew, house, 8
Shrew, Savi's pygmy, 8
Shrew, South-east Asian white-toothed, 8
Siamang, 37
SIRENIA, 63
Sotalia borneensis, 68
Sousa plumbea, 68
Squirrel, black-banded, 31
Squirrel, black giant, 32
Squirrel, cream-coloured giant, 32
Squirrel, ear-spot, 31
Squirrel, grey-bellied, 30
Squirrel, Himalayan striped, 32
Squirrel, Horsfield's flying, 35
Squirrel, large black flying, 35
Squirrel, mountain red-bellied, 30
Squirrel, plain pigmy, 32
Squirrel, plantain, 30
Squirrel, Prevost's 31
Squirrel, red-cheeked flying, 35
Squirrel, red giant flying, 34
Squirrel, shrew-faced ground, 34
Squirrel, slender, 31
Squirrel, spotted giant flying, 35
Squirrel, three-striped ground, 33
SQUIRRELS, 29

Stenella malayana, 68
Suncus etruscus, 8
Suncus murinus, 8
Sundasciurus tenuis, 31
Sus barbatus, 59
Sus scrofa, 59

Tadarida plicata, 19
Talpa micrura, 7
Tamiops macclellandii, 32
Taphozous melanopogon, 17
Tapir, Malayan, 58
Tapirus indicus, 58
Tarsier, western, 22
Tarsius bancanus, 22
Teledu, 55
Temadu, 62
Tenggalung, 48
Tenggiling, 28
Tenuk, 58
Thecurus crassispinis, 41
Tiger, 45
Tikus ambang, 6
Tikus babi, 7
Tikus belukar, 37
Tikus buluh, 39
Tikus duri hitam-pudar, 39
Tikus kecil, 38
Tikus lembah, 38
Tikus menggali tanah, 7
Tikus mondok, 36
Tikus mondok ekor panjang, 38
Tikus rumah, 36
Tikus sawah, 37
TRAGULIDAE, 60
Tragulus javanicus, 60
Tragulus napu, 60
Tree-mouse, pencil-tailed, 39
Treeshrew, common, 9
Treeshrew, large, 9

Treeshrew, pentail, 10
TREESHREWS, 8
Trichys lipura, 42
Tupai akar malam, 10
Tupai belang tiga, 33
Tupai bukit, 30
Tupai bunga, 32
Tupai cerleh, 31
Tupai gading, 31
Tupai merah, 30
Tupai muncung besar, 9
Tupai naning, 34
Tupai pinang, 30
Tupai telinga kuning, 31
Tupai teratuk, 30
Tupai terbang ekor merah, 35
Tupai terbang merah, 34
Tupai terbang pipi merah, 35
Tupai tompok, 31
Tupaia glis, 9
Tupaia minor, 9
Tupaia tana, 9
Tylonycteris pachypus, 18
Tylonycteris robustula, 18

Vampire, Indian false, 17
Vampire Malayan false, 16, 17
Viverra megaspila, 49
Viverra tangalunga, 48
Viverra zibetha, 48
Viverra malaccensis, 49

Wa-wa, 26
Weasel, Malay, 54
WEASELS, 53
Whale, Bryde's, 65
Whale, Indian pilot, 66, 67
Whale sperm, 65
Whale, Stejneger's beaked, 65
WHALES, 64